LOST IN FRANCE

LOST IN FRANCE

DARON HOGG

AuthorHouse™
1663 Liberty Drive
Bloomington, IN 47403
www.authorhouse.com
Phone: 1-800-839-8640

First published by AuthorHouse   08/10/2011

ISBN: 978-1-4520-3073-9 (sc)

Printed in the United States of America

Contents

Prologue

I decided to write this book after many of my close friends prodded me to do so, I thought about it for a very long time and then decided, why not? and proceeded forward putting pen to paper . . . . in that old fashion way of writing in long hand . . . I guess rare in this time of technology . . . . So I started to write and was transported back to the 6 weeks I had spent in the South of France in 1983, as a 15 year old.

But would anyone really be interested in my story of prancing around the Cote de Azur dressed as Boy George? It was extremely cathartic releasing the ghosts of my past as I spent nights scribbling my memories whilst chain smoking and drinking myself to death . . . I felt like one of those old fashioned authors! Once I had started, there was no stopping me . . . . it flooded out of me upon the paper, I just couldn't put the pen down (or my glass), the ash tray filled up. I laughed out loud, I cried tears so I could no longer see the page. I felt 15 again at certain moments. Not really having a care in the world . . . I was 'Lost in France' once more.

I then rang my close friend Suzi Skelton and asked for her advice, and she would edit and type the whole manuscript up for me. She agreed thankfully and we were on our way. If Suzi had said no, I don't think that I would of got this book finished. So now I would like to thank

Suzi for all her hard work, and blistered fingers from typing. (Sorry Suzi!)

I would also like to thank my Mum who wasn't so sure about the whole process and thank her for all her love and support over all the years, no matter what I got myself into, there is nothing like a mothers love.

The people mentioned in my book have had there names changed for copyright and privacy. They know who they are, and I thank them as well for the adventure that made this book possible. I am still in contact with some of that summer gang, but have not told them what I was up too, I did ring both Randy and Milly, as I needed them to jog my memory a couple of times. I had a few press cuttings to use for reseach, as on my return to the UK, I made some of the gossip magazines of the time. So what could I do when everything was falling into place . . . I had to write.

Lastly I would like to Thank You for picking up my book and reading it, and not think of me as a bad naughty 15 year old boy. But as just a 15 year old who wanted an adventure. And yes!!! I did.

I was 'Lost in France' . . . . 'Lost in a Dream' . . . . 'Lost in my own, made up World'.

Milly has an idea!

The telephone rang, "It's Milly." said Mum. "Hi Milly are you ok?". "Yes I'm fine". said Milly. "I have had an idea! How about all of us go to the South of France for the season? We won't need much money."

"How much do you think we need then?" I replied. "Oh! about £100" she answered. "I better ask my Mum though."

My Mum had just been through a divorce and had bought a bungalow in Saltdean, and I was a bit too much of a handful for her right now, so the idea of six weeks without me, she might be in her element.

"Mum, can I go to France for the season with Milly, Randy, Katy, Carol and Zoé".

"Well, I will need to speak to Milly, Daron! Remember you've only just turned fifteen . . ."

"Hold on Mum I'll call her back," "Hi Milly, it's me . . .".

Milly came around the next day to speak with my Mum about 'The French Trip'.

"We will be staying in Ste Maxime, just a few miles along from St Tropez and we will hopefully be able to get some work doing something or other. We will be camping on the beach under the bridge—It's fine everyone stays there; and it's FREE, so we dont have to pay for a campsite".

My Mum had an overnight think about about Milly's proposal. The next morning Mum broke the news to me . . . ." Daron, you can go, on the understanding that Milly looks after you, and for the trip will be kind of your guardian. But you must keep me informed of where you are, when you arrive and keep me up to date about everything! . . . Promise?".

I grab my Mum and give her the biggest hug and kiss ever, as I so wanted to go on this trip. "Thank you Mum!".

"Ooh, just one thing Mum . . . can I have some spending money?" I asked.

My Mum agreed in knowing smile that I was going to ask that of her, of course Mother's know their kids too well and so often know the next question before we do.

All set, I'm going to France for the Summer Season!

I was going with and was part of a Brighton based cabaret act . . . . The Allstars, we did shows impersonating Popstars. Milly was 21, with long blonde hair and very street wise. Randy was also 21, gay and very pretty, born in Zanzibar. Carol was 20, very tall with huge breasts and extremely outgoing personality. Katy was 19, and Carol's cousin, and much quieter, but also very pretty with long black hair with bright red streaks. Zoé was 21, and had gone to the same school as Milly, she was half Turkish and half English, and just a little bit crazy—Well, in fact, we all were somewhat crazy.

We are The Allstars, of course. A mixture of sweet and sour and sunshine!

I was 15, and I never attended school, (I hated school), but I loved Boy George, gay and all dressed up to the nines. I wore second hand clothes and 'Rags' my Mum always said. "Why do I have to wash your 'Rags' and hang them on the washing line? Goodness knows what the neighbours think?".

"oh, sod the neighbours" was my response.

The Meeting at
Lincoln Gardens.

It was a hot July in 1983, we all went around to Randy's to meet up to talk over the details of our trip to France. "We better ring up Jimmy to tell him that we are all going away" I said.

Jimmy Jones was our manager, he was a band promoter and ran the New Regent in Brighton. It was a band and bar venue at the bottom of West Street.

"Hi Jimmy", said Milly. "The Allstars are all going to France for about 5-6 weeks for a holiday, so we wont be availible to do any gigs for a while. We will ring you when we get back! Have a great Summer Jimmy" we all shouted from behind Milly.

"How are we going to get to France then? I asked.

"By boat . . . STUPID!" said Zoé . . . . Laughing at me.

"Yeah, I know that, I didn't think were going to swim the English channel! STUPID!" I retorted laughing too. "But how are we going to get down to the South of France?"

"We are going to hitchhike in two's." answered Milly.

"Oh! . . . Hitch? . . . mmmmm, oh well!" I mumbled. I had only hitched in the UK before and my French wasn't up to much, with me missing so much school, so I was a little apprehensive. Everyone used to hitch in the 80's, so it was not too big a deal, and we would be in pairs, so I guess it would be ok.

Milly and Zoé had been to the South of France before, and had not had any problems in hitching down there.

"When are we going?" piped up Katy. She never said much, but always looked pretty. I liked Katy.

"The end of July." answered Milly. "The season will be up and running and if we stay for the 5-6 weeks, it'll be time to come home as the season will be finishing and Daron will be back in time for school.". I look at her with a frowning face . . . Bloody School, I think! Go back to school . . . BACK TO SCHOOL, BACK TO SCHOOL, BACK TO SCHOOL, the shop windows were full of that already and I hadn't even broken up yet! Going back to school had never even entered my head, Damn School . . . . I Bloody HATE it!

I was so excited! I had never been out of the UK and was so estatic to be going to France . . . and without any family members to prevent me from having a FUN time!

A week went by, only a few days left until my great big adventure in France. I borrowed a ruck sack and sleeping bag from a friend, and packed my essentials, my walkman with cassettes, PASSPORT, towel, toothbrush/soap etc, my 'RAGS' and not forgetting my Boy George costume and wig. Well you never know if I get bored I can put that on, everyone always says I look like him in my get up and slap (make up). Must not forget the make up and crimpers then I think . . . . and of course my spending money. I am so, so, excited . . . I just couldn't wait. Why do days seem so long when you are waiting for something to happen, and disappear so quick when you are there?

OFF WE GO!

We had arranged to all meet early at the Palace Pier to get the bus to Newhaven. Randy was late as usual. Carol was all packed and ready for the off. Zoé all packed and diddery. Katy was early, all together and crimpers packed. Milly all packed and ready for anything. And myself was all packed and desperate to get going on our big adventure.

"Right, has everyone got their passports? said Milly "Yes!" we all shout at her in unison. "Money?", and again we all echo a loud "Yes!"

The bus arrived and we all piled on. As the bus went through Saltdean I looked over and peered at my home with my Mum in there all alone and without me. "She'll be alright" I said to myself. I mean, well at least my sister will go and visit her and she has got a dog to keep her company. She wont be too lonely. She has been through hell with me, not going to school etc, having a fight with the deputy headmaster and then being sent to a special school for naughty boys. "Oh . . . . stop it Daron!" I think to myself . . . "Mum will be JUST fine!"

We arrive in Newhaven and bought our tickets one by one. I think we got same day return tickets because they were a hell of a lot cheaper than buying an open return. I don't even know to this day, years later if an open ticket is availible?

All aboard, we set down our ruck sacks. The warm sun beating down on us and the sea glistening with what seemed more sequins than my Boy George costume. We sat there on the ferry's smoking deck puffing away. We were on our way. We were sailing to France.

Some of us had our cameras, so few snap shots of us all on the deck were taken and then we hit the bar. I had to hide as I was underage and not meant to be partaking of alcoholic beverages. But I looked 18. I had a pint of lager, not a shandy, and a cheese and ham roll.

"ARE WE THERE YET!" I wined. Everyone turned round and glared at me,

"Shut up Daron!".

A couple of drinks later, we decided it was time to decide who we were going to pair up with for the hitchhiking part of the journey. So it was, Carol and Randy, Milly and Katy, and I went with Zoé. I was a little stunned as I had assumed that I would be traveling with Milly as she had promised my Mum that she would look after me. I thought she was my best friend and there she was abandoning me within hours of setting off. "Sod it!", I didn't mind too much Zoé was capable of keeping an eye on me I wasn't a baby after all. I wasn't scared . . . I was far too excited!

The horn of the ferry sounded, it answered my question . . . WE WERE THERE!!! We had arrived in France, We were in Dieppe.

Before we split into our pairs, we got a few things straight.

We were aiming to meet up in Ste Maxime, Near St Tropez, Cote de Azur and we all were to meet under The Bridge on the beach.

It was kisses goodbye to my four other fellow travellers and off we set. Zoé and I decided it might be a good idea to at least buy a map of France to see how far we could go with each hitch, and if the offered journey would take as nearer to our destination. We sat outside a café in Dieppe having a coffee and studying our map. Bloody Hell, it was along way we had to travel. I couldn't believe it!

We decided we needed a piece of cardboard, to make ourselves a sign to use for hitching, so I went to the local fruit shop, I asked in English, I had not even attempted to try in French yet, if they had an old cardboard box I could have? They did. I rummaged in my bag for a pen and on the ripped up box we made two signs saying SOUTH, the pen didn't show up enough so I got out my black eyeliner and wrote mine, it ended up blunt so Zoé wrote hers with bright red lipstick. At least it was colourful. WE paid for our drinks and made our way to the lorry park where all the lorry drivers from the ferry were departing from for their destinations all over France.

"Voulez vous South, South, South?" waving our arms to attract attention and shouting.

"Wee (oui), wee (oui) I go-z South onlyz 100km, you-z both can-z (h)ave ze lift, I pleaszed to take of you with moi for-z ma journez, fromz Anglettre Wee(oui)?

"Wee (oui), mercy (merci)" we said politely. Zoé and I have our first lift on our intrepid expidition. Yes, we are on our way . . . . Off we go . . . The South of France here we come! FANTASTICO!!

In France.

Zoe and I sat in the cabin of the lorry alongside the driver, I remember him being very polite, He did his best to speak with us in English. It was one of those cabin's that had a bed installed at the back so he must of been a long distance driver who had to stop when he had done his daily quoter of driving hours. But who cares? He was taking us our first 100km or so.

"Youz like a drinkz?" he asked. We were gasping, "Yes, please." we replied.

"I haz beacoup de bottlez of ze French beer in ze back" he pointed behind him. Zoe and I got a couple out to drink. It was warm, the sun was shining, the driver was very accomodating and spoke a kind of English we could understand at least. The windows were open, the radio blared out with music. As we drove through France, drinking and smoking no way was I going to complain.

Zoe was very funny, coming out with silly jokes, bless him he didn't understand, but still he laughed with us, he was very nice I thought, not you normal run of the mill, sterotype of a truck driver that you would imagine. It was time for a toilet break and a leg stretch. We were half way through our 100km with him, quite near to Paris I believe. I think he kind of had his eye on Zoe, but he wouldn't be rude and make a pass at her, as I think he might of thought that Zoe was my older sister.

The sun was getting warmer. Well, it was July. I could feel the wind and sun on my face as I leaned out of the cab's window. Another hour went by,

"I thinkz ze have toz go off on to ze road for tripz to the south now!" the driver said. He pulled over and shook our hands, and as we climbed down he passed us our ruck sacks. As he drove off we waved goodbye. We were alone again, with only each other for company, it was still warm and still sunny, It must of been about 6 o'clock.

"Zoe, shall we carry on or camp here for the night?" I asked.

"It's busy for this time of day, let's carry on." So we did. Out came the cardboard signs, with the words the south emblazoned upon them. After about 10 minutes we got our next ride, we were very lucky in being picked up so quick. A sweet little old man took us the next 20km, he didn't speak English and of course we couldn't speak French. It was a quiet little journey, he smiled at us, we smiled back and he offered us a cigarette each. And before we knew it that 20km disappeared. He pulled over we got out and off he went, we were ready to find our next hitch.

I think by now, by looking at the map we were in the main region, thumbs out, signs out, we hoped our next lift didn't take too long. Within minutes a car with a young couple with a baby pulled over to give us a lift. We got in the back either side of the baby in its seat. The couple spoke English, the baby was fast asleep. We were tired too, a mixture of traveling and I think the fact we'd been drinking in the warm weather. They took us 50-60 more km's, I guess we must of been nearly half way down France by now.

We were left near a garage, the sun was going down and we were hungry. We made our way to the garage we had been left by to grab something to eat. We bought ourselves cheese rolls and some water. We wondered if we should carry on or camp out around here for the night.

"Sod it", I said "lets keep going, we've been so lucky so far". We were extremely lucky within what seemed like seconds an old lady picked us up. Lift after lift, old men that stank of tobacco and garlic and young dudes. But we were not complaining though we were more than half way across France and it hadn't cost us a franc!

"Let's call it a night" Zoe sighed. I agreed I was knackered. We found a spot to the side of the motorway near a little wood, so the trees would give us some shelter. We were pretty near another service station, once the morning came we could brush our teeth and wash before venturing out on the next stage of our journey. We set up our camp, and then Zoe went along to buy some bits and pieces and use the bathroom. Once she returned I wandered along to get something to eat for the evening, use the toilet, wash and clean my teeth. I got some crisps yet another cheese roll and a very big bottle of water, well you couldn't drink the tap water.

"Night Daz!" "Night Zoe!". We sounded like the family in The Waltons. We spent the night under the stars . . .

Still on the Motorway.

Zoe and I woke up to the sound of birds, the heat of morning sun and cows staring at us over the fence from the next field. "What's the time Zoe?" I asked. "I think it's 6am-ish, "she replied "I haven't changed the time on my watch." Nor had I and quite frankly I didn't care anyway. It was the most beautiful of mornings, The sun was scorching already. The traffic was beginning to build up on the motorway, caravan's lorry's and cars. There seemed to be a fair amount of people around at this early hour in the car park of the service station. Right beside our home for the previous night.

I wrestle myself out of my sleeping bag just like a butterfly emerging from its cocoon. I stand up and stretch my wings, sorry still thinking of butterflies, I mean my arms. Right it's time for a wash etc and breakfast . . . . wonder what that will be? Yep, you've guessed it another cheese roll and a bottle of water.

"I think it's good we are setting off so early," Zoe declared. "It would be rather fantastic, if we could make it all the way to Ste Maxime before dark tonight."

Zoe and I did not really have much of an idea where on earth we really were in France, in fact we could be absolutely anywhere! But we felt and kind of knew we were on the right track. It was so damn hot we had to be getting near the south. Face and body washed, teeth brushed, toilet needs over and done with, cheese roll eaten we made our way to the edge of the motorway once again, all ready to hitch. The start of our hitching day was not starting as well as the previous day. It took ages to get a lift, as all the people were probably on their way to their own holiday/vacation. And did not want to stop for us, desparate to reach their destination, just as much as we did. An hour later . . . . No luck . . . . No lift . . . . and still no sign of one. Then finally as the afternoon kicked in we got our first step on the days journey. It was a case of 20km here and 10km there, it wasn't really happening for us that day. No one was stopping for us.

"Maybe we will get a lift by from the over night drivers?" sighed Zoe. We did manage a few more pick ups, and to carry regardless of the time. We were getting pissed of now, why on earth were these drivers not stopping for us? I wondered if the rest of the group were having the same difficulties or were they there yet and wondering where the hell we were? Finally we got another lift. Thank God! Through this journey we took it in turns to nap. Zoe would have a little sleep, I would sing along to the radio, then I'd nap, Zoe would sing and so on. One of us awake the other sleeping so to protect each other. At last we were on our way once again. It couldn't be too far now could it? When we had reached the end of that hitch we had absolutly no idea where we were and we were so so tired.

We sat at the side of the service station we had been dropped off at, for about half an hour until a lady picked us up, no conversation here again a language barrier, but she did smile at us. She was driving to Montpelier, and we knew that was definitly in the south. Zoe took out the map and had a bit of a fight with it before she could look at it and gauge our potion on it. We had made it futher south than we had antisipated. It was nightime in Montpelier, so Zoe and I decided to look for a bar for a beer. We were not talking that much because all we really wanted is to be back together with the rest of the group.

We sat at the bar in the centre of town wondering should we carry on tonight. Yep, we would we were so near now why wait? We were not that tired. Just a little anxious. We walked along the main street of Montpelier and stuck out our thumbs and started hitching right then and there. When people stopped we said with our silly french accents "Ze Motorwayz, St Tropez, South, mercy (merci). Before long we had managed a couple of short pick ups and were back at the motorways side. We just wanted a UFO to whisk us up and dump us in Ste Maxime and wham bam thank you mam we'd be there. But of course life is never that simple.

Suddenly from nowhere a large truck/lorry pulled up beside us, the driver was going to Marseille, at last our luck had changed. It was dark, and the air was humid and we were feeling very sticky now. "How far is Ste Maxime from Marseille?" I asked. The driver answered in perfect English "About 50km on the motorway, don't worry I'll leave you on the right route for your destination." "Merci, merci . . . Thank you".

Later that evening Zoe woke me up, while I dozed in the Lorry's cab. "Daron, wake up, we've arrived in Marseille". God, I thought we haven't got much further to go now. The driver had to divert because of a pile up after an accident on the motorway and took us directly into the middle of Marseille. He shook our hands and wished us luck (in the most sexy French voice I had ever heard) and told us to take care. We in return we thanked him for picking us up and delivering to Marseille. Here we were in the centre of the city, it was very busy and we had no idea what to expect. The people around us didn't seem to be French or tourists for that matter. They seemed to be Algerians or Morrocans we seemed to be in a ghetto of sorts. I was starving and so was Zoe, we decided to go and grab a kebab as there was a mulitude of kebab shops around us. I really enjoyed it, it was Fab! At last a hot meal and not a cheese roll. My first in 2 days. After two beers we felt much better and contented. And even more determined to reach out destination. We walked along until we came to a river, and started to hitch yet again. In less than a minute of sticking out our thumbs a car pulled up beside us. Inside were two middle aged French guys and they took us along to the motorway. It wasn't far but we were back on track. We were pleased, we were nearly there or so we thought . . . . !

Where's Zoé?

Zoé and I sat beside the motorway, within a few minutes the people that stopped and tried to talk to us, but we could not understand, so our journey was heading nowhere really fast. It was yet another warm, very warm day. Zoé wore just a T-shirt and I wore only a vest on our upper bodies. We were being to catch the sun, so we were now getting a healthy glow instead of the pasty whiteness of being night people. Even so we were dog tired and pretty miserable.

A car pulled up, driven by turkish looking guy, well he could of been North African or even French, I couldn't say to be honest. He parked the car and spoke a smidgion of English to us. I didn't really trust his manner. I had some kind of mad vibe. He asked Zoé if she would go for a beer with him and to smoke some hash . . . . To my utter suprised Zoé agreed. She turned to me and said "Stay here I won't be long, I'm just going to get some beers for us". I was worried. But I knew Zoé wouldn't abandon me, or run away with someone she had no clue about. Zoé just wasn't like that. So off she went with this strange guy (well in my eyes he was very odd). I had Zoé's passport and bag, money . . . . in fact all her belongings. So she wasn't going far.

An hour passed, the sweat was begining to drip from my forehead. Where the hell was Zoé and where was the strange man she left with. Then he suddenly appeared beckoning me, "You come, you come!"

"Where's Zoé?" I replied.

I was more than a bit frightened, the man took me to the train station in Marseille.

"You wait here! I get your friend."

So I waited, and waited and I waited.

Another hour passed by and he returned once more, but again without Zoé. My mind was racing with thoughts by now.

"Ok we go" he said.

What the Fuck, I thought. "No, where's Zoé?"

"She come, she come" he answered.

I went with him, but feeling very anxious. He took me back to the side of the motorway and again told me to wait, while went to fetch her.

My mind was working overtime by now, all I could think was Oh! my God! He's Killed Zoé, and now he's going to kill me!

There I stood all alone. This was the worst thing, stranded somewhere in France, on my own with both Zoé's and my belongings . . . I had everything we owned.

I sat down upon the grass verge, and sat, I was sleepy, and I think I must of dozed off for 10 minutes at a time, and still no sign of Zoé. Before long it was morning . . . No Zoé. I had waited for for 12 hours now. I felt sick to my stomach. Nothing! No sign of anything. No Zoé, No strange man . . . . No nothing. What on earth was I supposed to do now? The thoughts of earlier where echoing around my mind. Zoé's DEAD! and he's going to come back and kill me next. There was nowhere to hide. I was stuck on the side of the motorway. It was baking hot, the sun beat down and I was sweating with heat and worry. I stayed awake all night and Zoé had still not returned.

I decided to carry on without her, to hitch to meet up with the rest of the group. I'd take all our stuff. I stuck out my thumb and very soon got a lift. They took me about 5km, and bit by bit I hitched further south. I got many lifts 2-3km here and there . . . I had enough. My mind was reeling, I couldn't work out what was going on? I went through many emotions. sad, angry, scared. All I could really do was get to the others in Ste Maxime. And report to the police that Zoé was missing. If I'd ever get there that was. If I was still alive!

It was early evening when I got my next lift. It was with an older man, he was bald and quite fat, a little buddha. He spoke ok English. I told him everything that happened. He told me to report it to the police. I had no idea of the French police's telephone number. I couldn't even remember where I had lost Zoé. Which of course I do now in hindsight, as I worked it all out on the map. The man said he was tired and said that he needed to nap. He then asked me if I was hungry? To which I told him I was. He said that he would book into a motel for a few hours and buy me something to eat, and then I would be able to freshen up with a shower or bath, and then have a little sleep too. God, I really needed that.

We checked in to a motel, it was still the afternoon. He said he had been driving all night as the roads were a lot quieter then, and like me he too needed a shower. He ordered room service . . . hot food, it was some kind of stew, a bottle of wine and a pudding. I ate so quickly and knocked back my glass of wine. Then I went for a shower, the warm water cascading over my dirty, smelly body. It felt wonderful.

He asked me to lay down next to him, I didn't really have much of a choice. There was only one bed in the room.

Anyway he didn't give off that kind of vibe the strange man Zoé had left with. I didn't feel he was going to kill me. After all we had been seen together as we booked in, and by room service.

As we lay there he started to mastarbate, Oh my God I thought . . . now what I got myself into? He made me do the same and that was it, he did try to kiss me . . . but I wouldn't let him.

All I wanted to do at this point was go home. Be safe and sound in my own bed. At home with my Mum and the dog. Drinking cups of tea. I hated France! I hated Men!

I hated myself . . . . I just wanted to die!

In the meantime, Milly had gone to the local police station in Ste Maxime, because unknown to me Zoé had already made it there without me. Zoé had told her about what had happened and I think Milly must of been beside herself with worry as she was meant to be my guardian for the trip. She must of been shitting herself. No Daron! What would she tell my Mum? The police had to make contact with the British Consel to inform them I was missing. That I could be anywhere between Marseille and Ste Maxime. It was doing some reseach many years later that I found out the consel had telephoned my Mother to actually tell her I was missing. Her baby boy daron was AWOL. There was nothing she could do at this point but pray that I was going to be ok, and that I would be reunited with my fellow travellers . . . . VERY soon. Poor Mum! Poor Me! Poor all of us!

Nudist Beach.

The fat balding bastard dropped me off at the motoway roadside, after he had had what he wanted. I didn't care anymore, I just wanted to get to the others, to back with the people I knew in Ste Maxime. To find Zoé and the others, to speak to the police and fly home to my Mum.

I started to hitchhike again, I had realised that I was not that far from Ste Maxime now. The heat was getting unbearable, the sweat was dripping off me completly.

I felt like a donkey, laden with both mine and Zoé's baggage. A rucksack on each shoulder.

My next pick up was a young French man of about 19. I thought he looked ok, but I was begining not to trust my own judgement. Hopefully he wouldn't kill me, or molest me . . . . and even if he did I had nothing else to lose. I had already lost my friend, not a clue where I am, I'd had some fat old arsehole try to rape me, my life was probally finished anyway.

The young man said that he would take me all the way to Ste Maxime, so I got in the car and off we set. The car was like being inside a tin can on the stove. It was boiling hot. He asked me if I fancied a paddle in the sea to cool off. THE SEA, at last we were on the coast. I agreed it seemed like a good idea. At last I was on theCoté du Azure. He parked up the car. I rummaged in my rucksack for my towel, but also took all the baggage of Zoé and mine with me, just in case. Yes, I was getting paranoid. I didn't want him driving off with our stuff, passports and money. He guided me down to this beautiful sandy beach, there were loads of people there. Suddenly I realised that everyone, Mum's. Dad's, Grannie's and Granddad's, even the kids were naked, it was a nudist beach. I had never been on a nudist beach before, even though Brighton had one, which opened 1979, I'd never been. But what could he do to me in the open air with people everywhere. After all it's only a dip in the ocean. He then told me we were only about 30km from Ste Maxime now, in a place near Toulon. I felt so happy at last to be so near to my destination. We wadded out into the sea, the water was warm and cooled me down, and freshened me up. When we got out, he went to a kiosk and bought me a coke and an ice cream, it was so nice after the experiance of yesterday. I felt almost like an innocent child again. I sat there on the beach naked, I must say it felt very odd, and I did feel self concious and a little embrassed to say the least. Even though everyone around was stark naked too.

The guy then said" it's time to make a movez, if we are going to getz you to Ste Maxime before dark. I grabbed my towel and shoved it back into the rucksack, threw my clothes on and we made our way back to the car. Once we got there he started to mumble something I couldn't quite hear or understand. Then he turned to me and said "Take off your trousers". What the hell, went rushing through my mind" No, I wont, I thought you were my friend". He wouldn't have it,

"I thought you were going to take me to Ste Maxime, not molest me after all I told you." He opened the car door and threw my bags out and drove off. I picked up a large rock to throw at his car, but something held me back, Thank

God or he may have killed me. I was begining to wonder if I had a neon sign above my head saying "ABUSE ME", it certainly felt as if I did.

I walked back down to the seafront, lit a cigarette and burst into tears, I cried and I cried, I could no longer hold back my emotions. I sat there chain smoking, lighting one after another, when I heard a car pull up behind me.

It was a young lady with the most piercing blue eyes I have seen to this day, and long blonde hair. She spoke with a very sexy French accent and asked if I was okay and where did I need to be. I told her Ste Maxime, apparently it was only 8km away. That guy had lied about how close we were as well as attempting to abuse me.

"I'll take you" she answered. I got into her car after throwing the bags in the back seat. We chatted, about what I really can't remember, but I do remember watching the signs pass by, Ste Maxime 7km, Ste Maxime 5km, Ste Maxime 3km, then 1km. And Finally Ste Maxime . . . . it was twinned with some town, whatever . . . wherever . . . I didn't care. I had finally got there. She took my hand, smiled very sweetly and told me to be VERY careful in future. I swear she must have been an Angel sent to me at my lowest point. She drove off, tooted her horn and I never saw her again. If she wasn't an Angel she was most definatly an Earth Angel.

I was on the beach road, I looked to my right the sun was glistening on the sea, and then I saw it . . . THE BRIDGE . . . . The Bridge in Ste Maxime, Cote de Azure.

I was there!!!!

Saint Maxime.

As I walked over to the bridge, I saw the bridge went over the sand on to the beach. I hurried down the stairs, and stood there and looked all around me. Where was Zoé? Where were my friends? I looked out toward the sea, and there I spotted a fine pair of Boobs bobbing up and down on the waves . . . it was Carol.

"Carol!" I screamed out to her at the top of my voice. She looked, I cried, I dropped the heavy bags I'd been carring and ran over to her, wadding through the water as fast as I could. Then Randy and Katy appeared as if from nowhere.

"Where the hell have you been Daron?" they asked. I didn't care I was finally with my friends . . . ." Where's Zoé?" I asked with a very worried tone in my voice. They informed me that Zoé had turned up a day earlier, but now had gone back to the motorway to look for me. She had believed that I had left her on her own. But it had been the man who had deliberatly split us up. Poor Zoé she was back on the motorway looking for me and no doubt worried sick. "Where's Milly?", I asked and was told that she was down the police station, reporting the situation. Shit! . . . I thought . . . I hope my Mum doesn't find out. She will probably be going mad with worry! We all went to the police station to tell them I was safe and sound, and here! But I thought it was best I didn't tell them all I had been through just now. As the Police could do very little about it anyway. We rescued Milly from the police Station and returned to The bridge to wait patiently for Zoé's return. The Police telephoned my Mum to let her know that I was safe. Zoé rejoined us later that evening, we hugged . . . . we both had thought the other had abandoned the other! But she was the one who had left me! Why had the man split us up? Only God knows why now! But thank the lord Zoé was a strong woman.

At last we were all together, all six of us. And we were ALL safe! My brain was fried, and doing overtime and just wouldn't switch off . . . . Just think if I had been killed, or if Zoé had . . . . or just imagine . . . IF . . . . IF . . . . IF . . . . !!!!!

At last I fell asleep under The Bridge!

Manshake!

We all slept like logs that night. Our big worries were over at last! Our camp was under The Bridge. Now in the light of morning we could now begin our holiday. It was a boiling hot day, Katy and myself ventured up to the supermarket to some food . . . bread, pate and gallons of water. I was extremely quiet, I guess it was the aftermath of the preceeding few days of trauma. I mentioned it to the others, and they were really quite concerned, it was the sudden realisation I was only 15 years old. it kind of at last hit them smack bang in the face, and I think they felt very guilty. But it wasn't really their faults. It had just happened . . . such is life . . . or C'est la vie as they say in France! As we wandered through the lovely little town that was Ste Maxime, I felt better, it was a beautiful little place, there were market stalls, cafés, bars, people on roller skates and a sense of everyone enjoying themselves. It was Summer, it was hot and it was the south of France. People from all over the world were there on their Summer Vacations enjoying themselves, a smile on everyones face.

There was fresh fruit . . . . grapes, lemons, limes, there was fresh bread, clothing, everything you could wish for in this outside market. I was on holiday . . . . . at last!

The last few hellish days began to finally subside backwards into the back of my mind. And slowly being forgotten. I ventured into a tiny postcard shop, bought a card and a stamp for England, then sat down outside in one of the street cafés for a coffee with Katy to write to my Mum.

> Dear Mum,
>> Arrived safely, all here, weathers wonderful,
>> It's soooo Hot!
>> We are living under The Bridge.
>> It's beautiful here,
>> Love you,
>>> Daron xxxx.

I found a postbox and sent the postcard to my Mum, hoping it would ease her mind when it arrived. I did'nt want her to think anything had gone wrong on the journey down here. Katy and I walked back to The Bridge, we all sat upon the beach and devoured the breakfast of French bread and pate.

It was a lovely day, we all swam in the sea, played volleyball, chatted, laughed and relaxed sunbathing in the hot foreign sun.

By early evening we were all a bit sore from being in the glaring sun all day. Milly took us all to an area which was a kind of wash place, all in the open air. It was mainly for doing your laundry by hand, but we didn't care and we all stripped off and scrubbed our sore pink bodies and soaked in the wash basins. We were clean, I felt really, really clean.

"Let's go out tonight" said Randy "Go to a bar to celebrate being all here!".

So we all rummaged through out kit bags and got ready for a night on the tiles. All dressed up, lots of make-up . . . in fact I decided to put on my Boy George garb . . . the full works . . . . costume and wig . . . the whole look. we trolled off to an open air restaurant/bar we sat down at a table and on the table lay a 20 franc tip, we took it! then we ordered some beer, lit up a cigarettes and relaxed. there was a one man band who started to play, he was very good and played an acordian . . . it really added to the French ambience . . . he was also using his feet to press a drum beat, and playing the keyboards at the same time. He was clever and I liked him very typically French. I was amazed at the ability to do all those things at once.

A few drinks later, 'The One-Man Band' said "Ooooh look, itz Boy George . . . comez singz for us". I thought why the hell not. I pulled up Carol and katy, asked him to give me a beat, then started to sing, I sang Manshake a B-side to Culture Clubs, 'Church of the Posion Mind'. The words were easy, and what I couldn't remember I just made up! He added some keyboard parts and I think we sang a decent song, which of course sounded NOTHING like the original version. The café audience were all clapping and stamping their feet. They adored it. To think we had only come out to have a celebrationary meal, to eat supper and drink wine and here we were performing. I don't think anyone there expected to have a live show of Boy George and his backing girls!!!!

We carried on performing for about 15 minutes, the crowd went wild, they were all on their feet cheering and clapping. By this time everyone on the square had made their way to see what was happening in this corner. The outside of the restaurant was now surrounded. There was about 120 people in total. It was amazing!

I said to 'the One Man Band' it was all getting a bit rowdy we should go, so we bowed and left. We didn't pay for our drinks but somehow I don't think the bar manager minded as we had filled the place. "you comez again pleasez" . . . . "Of course" I answered.

We had people following us asking for autographs, which I naughtly signed as Boy George, well I didn't want to break their illisions that I was not really George. Why upset them?

I was enjoying having all that positive attention . . . . so much nicer than all the negative attention I had got on the motoway.

Shake me . . . Let's do it!!!!!

Losing my Identity.

In the morning the police woke us all up from our sleep, "You can'tz sleep erez". The police didn't want hitchhikers ruining their pretty town and making it look untidy . . . "Ok we go". We all packed up our bags and pretended to wander off, as soon as the police had gone from sight . . . . WE were back! They were not moving us . . . We were staying. Sodem!

Milly, Randy and I went off for our daily scrub in the washing tubs. Stripped naked, washing our hair and scrubbing themake up off our faces from the previous night. It was a glorious day again, really hot and it was still only about nine in the morning.

After our daily ablutions we followed the ritual of the daily visit to the supermarket for the water, bread, cheese and pate our basic breakfast.

"Where's Randy?" I asked as we came out. "Oh, he probably wanted something else or got lost in the supermarket" Milly giggled. After 5 mins we decided to go in and find him. Where we saw Randy being pushed into an office at the back of the store, by a number of security guards. He had been caught by them shoplifting. In France apparently you can not arrest someone if they are poor or foreign if it's food they are stealing. It's illegal? (Or something like that?) A funny French law.

So the security guys decided to give poor Randy a couple of punches in the face and told him never to darken the doors of this supermarket ever again. Poor Randy he was so scared.

We walked through town, Randy was truly shaken. We wandered past the restaurant that had been our stage the night before. Then suddenly from nowhere a man appeared and came up to us. He spoke very good English, and was carrying a huge camera . . . . just like the Paparazzi love to lug around. He said to us "Ooooo youz Boy Geogre's friendz, pleaze give him theze". They were photo's from the night before. "Maybe I take some good photos of youz all and ze Boy George soon?" We continued to talk with him and he said he would give us copies of the photos he took and even pay us . . . . something for our time! We liked that! To be paid and keep the photos . . . Fantastic! We told him in a few days maybe? I really wanted to give it a rest and try to enjoy my holiday, not put on make-up every night and parade around Sainte Maxime as Boy George everynight. It would be nice if people looked at me . . . . not me as Boy George. I felt like Daron was dissappearing into thin air and the spirit of Boy George had taken over me. Especially as now my English gang of holiday friends were now calling me George as well all the night before. Sometimes someone would screw up and call me Daron by mistake in front of a whole bunch of people that didn't know otherwise.

We said Goodbye to the photographer and told him that we would let Boy George know about the photo session. Even though George already know, because I was George, but in disguise as Daron.

We sat on the beach had our breakfast and covered our bodies with suntan cream. By this time we were getting very brown. We told the others about the photographer and showed the photo that he had given us. Carol and Zoé weren't so sure about having a photo session with him, they thought it would be risky! They thought that if I pretended to really be George it was some sort of crime. Fraud? Maybe it was ok? Who knows? That evening we took it easy. Just walking through the town looking at the shops. Everyone still looked at us. We could hear whispers and know many where thinking . . . they were with Boy George last night, they are his friends. When asked we told them he was at his hotel. Well he would if been if he really was here.

Later that evening, we got some cheap wine and a few beers, sat on our sleeping bags under the bridge chatting, smoking and drinking our plonk!

There were quite a few other hitchers from the UK there, they all knew i wan't Boy George and knew the story so far! We sat talking with them until the early hours, I most of dozed off, I was Knacked!

Donuts & Soda.

We were not the only one's from England sleeping under the bridge, but they always got up so early each morning about 7am. I guess they were trying to avoid being moved on by the Police. Our morning call every morning was the Police waking us up, they didn't want the real hotel holidaymakers seeing us camping under the bridge on the Cote de Azure . . . might lower the tone and make the beach look untidy . . . . he he!

I asked the early rising English why they rose so early and found out that they had got a job with a local firm selling Apple Donuts and Cold Soda Pop. "It's not bad money, we get a percentage for everything we sell, and sometimes we have sold it all in a matter of hours". I asked them where they sold them, and was told that they got dropped off in two's on all the beaches along the road from Ste Maxime to Cannes. "We have a large wicker basket with 50 apple donuts and about 50 cans of soda, anything from orange, cola, lemonade . . . . why don't you come along one morning and see if you can make a few francs? If you don't sell that much you can always chill out on the beach. We get picked up about 8am in the morning, and from our beaches 5.30pm and we get the cash there and then, no questions asked."

As a group we all had a disscussion and decided maybe we should all give it go. Well, it was a day out even if we didn't like it! Surely it couldn't be that bad, walking up and down the beach selling our wares. We all went up to the water hole to wash ourselves as we did every day. Then we ran back to the beach by the bridge and waited with the others for our pick up. And when it turned up it was a rusty old van . . . . and it was dead on 8am. The driver asked us if we had done beach selling before? We told them we hadn't, and he then told us that it could be quite hard at times, because some tourists came to the beach all prepared with the packed lunches and picnics. Some days we could sell out, others nothing at all. It was the chance we took, and only got money if we sold things as we were on a percentage. No sell. No pay. Also we were entitled to one donut and soda for our lunch. We thought why not . . . we would give it a go!

I ran down under the bridge to ask a few of the other travellers who lived under the bridge with us, to see if they would keep watch over our bags. They kindly said they would. I thanked them and charged back up to the top of the bridge. There were 10 of us altogether and the 2 English guys. In the van were big baskets full of freshly cooked apple donuts and a large cooler box each with the chilled fizzy drinks. Half a mile up the road the first 2 boys from Bedford got dropped off, "Bye . . . . See you later" . . . then another 2 were dropped off half a mile later . . . . then Randy and Carol got dropped off, then next it was Zoe and Milly . . . . myself and Katy were dropped off about a mile later. They told us we would be picked up about 5.30pm—ish! Adding "oooh watch out for the police!" "What? Why? "Katy asked "Because it's illegal to sell on the beaches here in France !"

"Oh, brilliant", I thought and mumbled under my breath, "that's all we need".

"And if the police do catch you they will confiscate all the goods and throw them into the sea . . . or just take them back them to the Police Station, ... Good Luck!"

Katy and I looked at each other, our faces both must of read What the hell had we got ourselves into? It was very, very hot today, the beach we had was pretty busy. There were all types there, kids playing ball, family's, young couples in love and allsorts . . . Liquorice ones selling illegal fare!

Katy decided to start at one end of the beach and said I should start the other end and we would meet up in the middle, and see how we were doing. I wished Katy good luck and we set off. I was shouting at the top of my lungs . . . ." Banya pomm, Cola, Limonade", all in my best French accent. "Wee, wee" I heard . . . Yes my first sale of the day, "Un Banya et un cola". "Merci" I replied. "6 francs". They paid me . . . I was so happy.

I met up with Katy in the middle like we agreed. She had done well, much better than me with my one sale . . . she had sold 5 donuts and 6 Sodas. But we still had 6 more hours to sell them in the blazing heat. We decided to stop, sit down and have a cigarette break and a can of pop from our stock! It was midday, the sun shone down upon us, i could feel beads of sweat turn to little streams dripping all down my body. I felt sticky. I needed a dip in the sea. When we met up I left my stock with Katy and did just that! It was wonderful, the water was warm and so refreshing.

A few hours had passed I had managed to sell another 7 donuts and 10 cans, but Katy was obviously better at selling than me . . . She had sold 20 donuts and cans. Maybe it was because a girl selling and they prefered to buy from a girl rather than a boy. Maybe I should of put on my Boy George outfit on . . . maybe I'd sell more? But by now it was too bloody hot! And maybe I would just be laughed at? We decided to share our other freebie can and eat our donuts. It was getting on in time. It was now about 4.30pm, and Katy had done so well, 30 of each she had sold! Me, I had 15 donuts and 20 cans. We sold a few more and then decided to call it a day and just sit on the beach for the last hour before the pick up. We waited at the point we were dropped at that morning. In the distance we spotted the rusty old van coming towards us, they said we had not done that well. I was livid, but i bit my tongue, I'd been up and down the bloody beach shouting my wares like some street seller in old covent garden market . . . . very My Fair Lady. I was knackered, we picked the rest of the gang on route back Ste Maxime. It seems Zoe and Milly had got caught by the Police, who had confiscated their stock and threw the donuts in the sea . . . . the fish would eat well today . . . . but the girls got no pay! The boys from Bedford did really well, they sold the lot. Randy and Carol didn't do to bad either. It seemed that Katy and I had the raw deal, our beach was tiny and not many people were on that beach buying our stock. The boys from Bedford said that they always had the best beach as they had been doing it for weeks now. As we arrived back at our bridge base, the English drivers sorted out our wages. I got about 5 measley francs . . . . all that hard slog for that! Sweet FA! When we got out of the van and walked back to the Bridge, Zoe and Milly told us they had sold quite a few items and kept the money . . . but had not let on to the drivers. How I wished I had thought of that!

The drivers asked us as we left if we would like to do it tomorrow, as it's the weekend and the beaches would be busy. we all declined . . . . Sod that for a laugh I thought. "No thanks, but thank you anyway "we replied.

As we arrived back under the Bridge, we realised how exhausted we were. My shoulders were really sore from where the webbing straps had dug into my flesh, and my skin was burnt to a crisp (remember this in a time where very few used sun screen). I went for a swim to ease my aches and pains, in the warm evening sea. I was tired and hungry. I was in real need of food and drink. Randy and I went up to the local kebab shop and treated ourselves to one with an ice cold beer. Bliss!

After stuffing ourselves we wandered the streets of Ste Maxime, along the cobbled lanes where we found a small market that was still open, it sold clothes, food and handicrafts. As we looked about I found a great t-shirt stall, and found one I really liked but it was way past my budget, I could feel it. Randy thought they were great too. "How much are they?" I asked. The lady who's stall it was told us that she came from Paris, she was really sweet. She designed the t-shirts herself. "ohh they are really nice" I told her. "Maybe I can buy one next week".

"wee, I'm here for 2 more weeks, I am Bridgette". "Hello", I laughed "I'm Daron and this is Randy". "Are you friends with Boy George" she asked. "Yes we are" answered Randy. "We are staying in the same hotel". "He is very good, I love his music" Bridgette said. "Maybe you will bring him here to say hello, Yes?" "Of course" I answered thinking to myself he would love these t-shirts . . . very him . . . or did I mean me . . . he he! A freebie for Daron (Boy George).

"Bye, we will see you tomorrow with George."

Randy and I walked back to the bridge. We all sat together talking about the events of the day. We lit a fire, supped on our cold beers. we listened to our walkmans, read books and chilled out. We were all very tired, sunburnt and we were happy. We watched the sun set over the Med, it was a delight, very beautiful and peaceful. I thought to myself I was really happy here.

Bridgette meets Boy George.

The Police woke us up YET again! Ooh sod this I thought, I can't bare being woken up like this every damn morning by the Police. It's not as if we have done anything wrong . . . we were only sleeping after all. Daily we would go through the ritual of packing up our bits and pieces and arrange them neatly in piles. It's not as if anyone was going to sit under the bridge instead of the beach, under a concrete bridge on the sand, we so not in anybodies way.

That morning I wore a huge pair of sunglasses and a rasta hat to protect my identity and set off for the market with Katy and Zoe. Well I thought I was going to blag a free t-shirt from Bridgette whilst pretending to be her idol Boy George. We walked through the market, and when we reached Bridgette's stall, there was another girl working there. I asked if Bridgette was around. The girl told us that it was her day off and she was keeping an eye on the stall for Bridgette. She told us that Bridgette had gone to Saint Tropez for a bit of shopping. "Could you let here know that Boy George popped by to say hello?" "Of course I'll tellz her you came, I am Annette". I then introduced Zoe and Katy as my backing singers. "I know" she replied "I saw you allz singing in the cafe bar. Can I have your autograph?" "Of course" I said. I delightfully signed her piece of paper.

"Bridgette will be backz laterz, could you come backz then, and we can all go for drinkz in ze bar?". I said "Ok we'll see you later at the cafe bar". Well I did want a free t-shirt . . . what was I like? I was so bored already wearing the stuff I had bought with me from England.

Katy, Zoe and myself walked round the small town for about an hour or so, then into the supermarket to buy our daily rations. We then headed back to base under the bridge. I took off my disguise, put on a pair of shorts and laid upon the sand . . . Daron's back again I thought to myself.

Money was getting a bit scarce now, we must of been hanging around under the bridge for 2 weeks. So we decided if we went to the Cafe Bar we would have to sip our drinks not gulp them down like water! Maybe if I wore the full Boy george . . . people might actually buy us drinks! Here's Hoping!

As the early evening was approching we decided that we would all make the effort to dress up this evening! Carol did my make-up, Randy sorted out my wig and Katy tied ribbons on to my costume . . . everyone wore their white dungerees with flip flops, the girls wore crop tops, did their hair . . . make up on . . . . now time to make our entrance in town.

We scrubbed up quite well, looked very stylish considering we were sleeping rough under the bridge on the beach. We parked our bums at the Cafe Bar, the one man band was there again. As we entered he waved at us and said "Boy George, Bonjour". We all waved back at him. We were getting quite a lot of attention by now, and we had only been there an hour. People were coming up and asking for our autographs and posing for their SnapShots.

The manager of the Cafe Bar came over to our table and offered us some wine. I told him that we didn't carry much money on us. Just like the Queen! to which he replied "Non . . .—it's for youz all Free . . . No Charge".

A couple of the girls from our group were a bit wary of this offer," What happens if he discovers that you are not George, he'll go apeshit!!!" "Oh Sod it!" I said "I never told him that I was!". It was something he assumed.

Within 5 minutes the manager returned carrying a bottle of Champagne and 2 bottles of 1 x red and 1 x white. We felt like Superstars! "It'z on zee houze pour youz" he said, we all thanked him with our little French . . . . "Merci, Merci beaucoup".

The market had packed up for the evening and the T-shirt girls joined our table. All the waiters were running about grabbing more spare chairs for our ever growing party.

Annette and Bridgette turned up with 7 bags . . ." We bring youz all a present" another "Merci" we all said. Inside each bag there was a t-shirt each. Milly looked confused and said "but there are only 6 of us!". Bridgette replied "The other is for your other friend, we all looked at each other . . . suddenly realising she meant me . . . Daron in my normal guise. Good I thought being greedy . . . I get two . . . na . . . na . . . na . . . na . . . na! Such a child I am at times. "Where is your other friend?" Bridgette asked. "Oh, he has a headache tonight!" I told them very quickly.

The Manager came over with another bottle of wine for us. I think he really liked us being there as it was helping his profits with everyone coming to his bar. We were causing quite a stir, photos and autographs!

The one man band asked me if I would sing a song again tonight. I agreed and with Katy, Zoe and Carol we made our way up to the little stage and started making up a song . . . it was to be a mixture of Culture Club songs. At times I just ad-libbed and sang Wooh alot and Yeah! But the audience didn't seem to mind, they were loving it. They clapped their hands and stamped their feet to the beat. After about about 10 mins. I took a bow and thanked the audience as we left the stage. I was gasping for a drink by now, the manager came over with another bottle of champas and thanked us one by one!

The photgrapher who we had met a few days before had turned up again. He reminded us of his offer of some photos. We all agreed to do the photos for him in a couple of days time. We told him that we would meet him at the jetty at 6pm on Tuesday. He added that he would pay for my time . . . . Fab I thought it would be great to have a few more francs for my empty purse.

The Cafe Bar was closing for the night as it was getting near 12.30 am. The manager came over to our table and thanked us, we offered to pay for our first round of drinks, but he wasn't having any of that. "Non, it was my privelage to have youz in my Cafe, youz will comez again Non?" We thanked him.

Annette and Bridgette asked me at which hotel I was at. I told them that I had checked out of my hotel and was living at the beach with the others.

"But Why?" she aked.

I said that I didn't like the comforts of the hotel, I had come here with my friends and being with them made me happier. I said that I had enough of hotels as my life on the road was hotel to hotel and I wanted to get back to my roots, and I actually liked slumming it and felt so free at the beach. They must of thought I had gone a little crazy . . . but I didn't care!

Bridgette and Annette were renting a villa and asked us if we would like to come and stay with them as they were still here for another 2 weeks selling T-shirts. We told them we consider their lovely offer, and let them know the next day. Bridgette told me that she had met a few session musicians who were here to work with a famous French singer. "You should meet them and I can arrange a big show for you?"

A big show!!! I thought . . . . Money . . . Money!!!!

We said our Goodbyes and told them we would meet up with them again tomorrow.

Now back to the Bridge for Bed!

Photo's and Villa.

Carol and Zoe didn't want to do the photo session, but Carol did offer to do my make—up for the shoot. Carol and Zoe had made some new friends of their own and were beyond fed up being woken up every morning by the police. And these new friends had said did they want to stay in their tents with them at the campsite. I wasn't keen on the group splitting up. But the girl's need the tent I guess. And they would only be 10 mins up the road from the bridge "You will be down here on the beach everyday, so we will keep on touch, won't we?" said Milly. "Of course we will, silly!" replied Carol.

Carol proceeded to make me up as George ready for the shoot. It looked really good. I was very brown by now and looked really healthy. Then after that Carol and Zoe got all their gear together and left us for the campsite . . . . it felt really odd.

So Randy, Milly, Katy and me headed off to the jetty to meet up with the photographer. He was already there, so well on time all ready with his big camera and tripod. "You guyz look wonderful!" he said. "Thank you!" we answered. He took photos of us on the beach, on boats and some back in town. We had such a ball, and great fun . . . I loved it I felt like a star! After the shoot which had lasted about 2 hours, the photographer took us for a beer at a Cafe. He said that the photo's would be ready by the next day, and that he woul give us copies of them to keep. Then he paid us for our time, I think it was about £50 in English money . . . we were rich!!!!

We divided the money between us and arranged to meet him tomorrow. We then headed off to have a drink through the market to a little bar we knew. Along the street on our way to the bar we bumped into Annette and Bridgette. They asked if they could join us there at the 'Blue Parrot Bar', we told them of course they could.

She then asked where the others were? We told her that they had gone to stay at the campsite to stay with some new friends, (all 3 of them!!!) We'll one of them was the other me! Bridgette asked us if we had thought about the offer they had made us the previous day of moving into the villa with them. "It's only 5 mins from here." said Annette. We looked at each other, and within a split second we agreed . . . the others had gone their way so why not? "Wee, we would love to, Thank You" I answered. Bridgette told us there were enough beds and that the villa had a lovely little garden to relax in. And that they had rented it for a further 2 weeks. "It would be wonderful to have you as our guests" added Annette. We told them that we would go and collect our belongings from the beach and join them back at the Blue Parrot in about 15-20 mins. We ran back to the bridge like a gang of young kids all excited at the prospect of sleeping in a bed again at long last. We threw all our bits in to our rucksacks in a hurried way. then we said Good Bye to our fellow travellers from Bedford. And asked them if they saw Carol and/or Zoe could they let them know that we had moved into the villa for 2 weeks. But that's only if they saw them, as we would be back tomorrow on the beach.

We were so pleased, warm cosy beds, a roof over our heads no longer the bridge and maybe a bath or real shower, I didn't realise how much I was missing the comforts of home.

We hurried back to Annette and Bridgette, and joined them at their table for another drink. Then Bridgette went off to get her rented car and we were off . . . villa bound! Five minutes until we reached our new home.

The Villa was hidden by trees, it wasn't massive, but it was a hell of a lot better than camping under bridge. Annette and Bridgette were to share the downstairs room and the four of us were upstairs sharing a room that had 2 double beds. Me and Randy would share one bed and Milly and Katy the other. We unpacked our bags and laid upon the beds . . . it was like resting on a cloud after the hard sand on the beach.

"Supper is ready!" Bridgette called up the stairs to us. We came down stairs and went into the garden, where our hosts had laid on a wonderful spread of pasta, salad and crusty french bread. Along with a couple of bottles of wine . . . . wow . . . this was better than our normal daily rations. I loved this, this really felt like a holiday now. Bridgette gave us a spare key so we had the freedom to come and go. They would have to leave early in the mornings to open their T-shirt stall. We could do as we pleased, but we must never forget to lock up when we left the villa. We agreed and said of course we would. It felt so good, and it was lovely that they trusted us, as we had only met a couple of times. Mind you they did think I was Boy George . . . so that probably was why they did. I mean having a star staying with you . . . well enough said.

We washed and put away the supper things and made our way up to our room. The beds were so soft and warm . . . it was heaven. I think I fell asleep as soon as I shut my eyes and my head hit the pillow. A matter of seconds. Oh to have a proper sleep and no police to wake us early in the morning. Blissss . . . . zzzzzzz!

Bridgette's Idea!

We all awoke from our slumbers to the sun beaming through the slats of the wooden shutters. Another glorious day under blue skies and in the French sun. We wandered down to the garden, where Katy had set the breakfast things out for our first morning at the villa. We had slept so well as it was now 11am, what a wonderful change not to be awoken by the local police. Annette and Bridgette had already left for their stall at the market. So it was just us, hanging out there at Villa. I wondered if Carol and Zoe were ok and were they at the beach waiting already for us? As a group, we decided that we should go to the supermarket to buy some things for the villa, as it wouldn't be fair if we ate all their food. So Randy would pop down to the bridge to tell the girls we had moved. Just so they didn't get worried that we had just packed up and disappeared. Well after his little inccident Randy was not now allowed into the supermarket.

Katy, Milly and I set out for the shops and today bought some pate, pasta, bread, wine, milk, beer, eggs & cheese . . . We couldn't buy too much as we didn't have a whole lot of money. But we thought that bringing in a few bits and bobs, we would seem as if we were not taking their hospitality for granted.

All the shopping done, we made our way back to the villa to put our wares away, we grabbed our swimming things, locked the door and hurried down toward the beach to meet up with Randy, Carol and Zoe. Carol and Zoe were pleased that we were now no longer stuck under the bridge and had somewhere else to live. They seemed very happy at the campsite, that they had their own tent and everyone was sharing everything with them from food to toiletries. We spent the whole day upon the beach, playing in the waves and chilling out reading. We were now holiday makers not longer Hitchhikers sleeping rough. We could pack up our towels now and do as we wished, not only move 10 yards to our beds under the bridge.

The day was really relaxing, there was no tension between us through being tired and stressed anymore. We laughed and joked and were a really happy band of people. It was a shame we were now split into 2 groups, but at least we were all safe and enjoying our Hols . . . we now only had about 2 weeks of it left . . . . so we needed to make the most of our time and enjoy it.

Before we knew it, it was 5.30pm-ish . . . time to collect our photos from the photographer. I couldn't go . . . as I was Daron right now and not in character. I was dressed casually not as Boy George . . . gosh it was getting very confusing. Who knew me as Daron and who knew me as The Boy?

So Milly, Randy and Katy went to pick them up while I stayed at the beach with Zoe and Carol. Within the the hour, they came back with the photos which were really good. We were really pleased with the results, and especially with the fact he had given us a whole set . . . about 40 in all, plus he paid us about 400 Francs (£40.00).

As we all parted company after our first true holiday maker day, we arranged to meet up with Carol and Zoe at The Blue Parrot Bar at 9pm that evening for drinky—poos! The rest of us meandered up toward the villa, I grappled in my bag to put on my Boy George Hat and glasses, Daron was no longer free, time to be larger than life and be BG! Just so I looked the part, I didn't want either Annette or Bridgette to find out the truth so I needed my disguise. We didn't want to be thrown out of being at the Villa and being comfortable now did I?

Annette and Bridgette's car pulled up, we all went into the garden with a bottle of wine and glasses and poured out some drinks. Katy was busy in the kitchen whisking up a meal of ommelette, salad and garlic bread. Katy was very house proud and I think the French girls really appeciated it that we had made some kind of effort. Katy's meal was delicious, she was a great little chef and it was so nice to be able to prepare stuff for ourselves. We sat and talked over another bottle of wine.

"I've had zee idea" Bridgette told us . . . ." I know you say that you dont have much money left, so why dontz you do a real show on here in Ste Maxime. She told us she could arrange a meeting with some session musicians and maybe you could do a gig at one of the many disco's on the sea front. "Yeah, that's a great idea . . . it really couldn't hurt now could it?" I replied and Randy and Katy agreed. "But we would need to rehearse with the band . . . give them my copy of the Culture Club cassette, so they can rehearse it for themselves."

"All done then" replied Bridgette "I will telephone the musicians and we can arrange a time tonight to meet up with them". I told her of our plans to meet up with Carol and Zoe at the Blue Parrot at 9pm that night, so maybe they could meet us there too. It would be great!" "Ok!" she answered "I willz ring them straight awayz", And off she went to do so.

So all was arranged for us to meet up with everyone at 9pm. I was really excited, me little ol' Daron was going to be singing with a proper band and would get some money in my pocket . . . WoW!. We spent the next hour getting ready for the meeting at the bar. I had to do my own make-up as Carol wasn't here, I slipped on my favourite Boy George shirt and hat on, Katy crimped her hair . . . . she was just so happy to be able to plug in, something beach life made impossible. Randy had twisted and crimped his dreadlocks, (he looked Fab as was normal) . . . we all looked FANTASTIC a proper's 80's band. After a couple more glasses of Vino we all piled into the hire car and headed down the road to our Band meeting at the Blue Parrot.

Annette bought a bottle of wine, and we pulled together to buy another, I was feeling a bit bolder by now I needed to be to have the gift of the gab to be Boy George. Zoe and Carol arrived then shortly after the musicians arrived too. We sat around our table for around 3 hours, the museo's buying bottle after bottle of wine along with the French girls. I felt a bit gulity, after I was meant to be the star . . . I should be buying and all I had was £30 to last me for the next 2 weeks.

I handed over my Culture Club cassette to the band, they said that they would go and rehearse the songs the next day, there were only 8 songs on it. But as they were professional musicians they would take no time to learn them. It was so exciting. Bridgette said that she would arrange to speak to the club manager on the front who ran The Saint and hopefully get us a gig for next week. Next week I thought . . . would I remember the words to the songs as I know longer had my tape? Of course no need to panic . . . Randy had a copy in his luggage too, I breathed a sigh of relief . . . . I would use his to practise while Annette and Bridgette went to the market to work. There was a tape player in the Villa so we could rehearse the songs and kind of routines.

It was gone midnight now, time to start out for the villa, time to go home . . . . so happy not to be sleeping under the bridge anymore . . . . oh a bed . . . . my kingdom for a BED! We kissed Zoe and Carol goodnight and goodbye and told them same place same time at the beach next day . . . We shook hands with the musicians and told them we would call them for another meet up in a few days.

As we drove back to the villa, I began to think . . . "God, what have WE GOT OURSELVES into?" It was getting pretty serious, Sod it! I'm on Holiday! I pulled myself together.

By this time I felt that Annette and Bridgette had twigged that maybe I wasn't really Boy George. But I thought I guess they don't really mind as it was probably all a bit of fun in their eyes! Well it was in mine too!

Bridgette had asked me a number of questions about my wig, I told her that I just wore it when I had to be myself as Boy George and not when I was hiding from the world . . . Not wanting to be reconised . . . another reason I was here in the south of France incognito with my friends. I hoped that she would believe my story, I felt it was a good enough excuse and she agreed it that it must be hard being famous and the need for an escape and no harassment. Would anyone want screaming fans all the time? Would you? OR would you?

Boy Darre[n] fools French!

By Tim Curran

● Young Hogg — he wa convince he was Boy George on the French Riviera.

● The real Boy George makes a entrance at Heathrow airport.

BRIGHTON'S Boy George lookalike Darren Hogg got a tremendous welcome in France — because they thought he was the real thing.

And he played along with it, even appearing at a plush night club as the pop star.

Darren slipped into the country with a Boy George wig and make-up neatly packed in his suitcase, so he didn't have the trouble with immigration that Boy George suffered last week at Nice airport.

In Nice, French officials told the Lancastrian-dressed star George they were not sure whether he was a boy or a girl — and they escorted him to stop to prove his innocence. George refused and it took two hours to prove that he was a well-known English pop star with a bizarre dress sense.

But Darren, who made his trip a bit earlier, decided to do his dressing up after he arrived, and was overwhelmed at the reception when he stepped out on the French Riviera.

The story of how he masqueraded as Boy George, and took everyone in, has only been revealed this week.

Darren told national magazine Titbits: "I dressed up for a laugh to see how people reacted. It was amazing. People were clamouring for his autographs and taking photographs.

"I never actually told anyone that I was Boy George. They just assumed that I was and I went along with it for a bit of fun."

Plush

Darren, 16, who was on holiday with the rest of the Brighton band of pop impersonators Equentie Alberto, even agreed to appear at a plush nightclub in St Tropez.

He says: "I was living the part so much I actually sang the Boy George instead of miming him. The others came on as my backing group. I forgot the words of one song, but no one twigged and the club paid us £250.

"I was worried that someone was going to discover the truth any minute," he says.

Boy George, left, ... right, Boy Darren ... wined and dined on the French Riviera.

LOOK-ALIKE DARREN PULLS OFF AMAZING HOAX

THE GREAT BOY GEORGE CON

...OOLBOY Darren ...has fooled hundreds of Boy George fans ...believing he was the ...ageous star. And he was besieged by ...graph hunters, wined and dined in top clubs on the French Riviera, posed for pictures and signed autographs and magazine covers.

...osed as the rugged sequinned singer, he sang in night spots as George — and took ...for one appearance.

...nother club offered me £100 a song, but I turned ...wn because my voice ...d up," says Darren.

...home in England, Darren, 16, is a member of the Brighton pop group ...rtie All Brighton who mimick pop stars while hoping their records.

...ran out the four other impersonators started their Ibiza holiday first year ...eeping rough on the ...t at St Tropez in the ...st France.

...says "I'd taken my own clothes.

BY TONY BASSETT

Boy George make-up, wig and clothes with me so I dressed up for a laugh to see how people reacted. It was amazing. People were clamouring for autographs and taking photographs.

"I never actually told anyone that I was Boy George. They just assumed that I was and I went along with it for a bit of fun."

He and his friends were so popular they estimate that more than £1100 was spent on 'them in drinks, food and gifts in four weeks.

Darren met a T-shirt designer from Paris, ... at her holiday home in Sainte Maxime.

He says: "She was so delighted to meet Boy George that she put me and some of the others up at her house.

...arranged a couple of unpaid gigs at a cafe and then got us a booking at the plush Le Saint-Hilaire de La Mer nightclub.

Adverts in a local paper and posters around the town announced: 'Exclusively in the Gulf of St Tropez, we present Liquidice All Sorts with, as guest, Boy George, singer of the group Culture Club.'

Darren says: "I was living the part so much that I actually sang as Boy George instead of miming him. The others came on as my backing group. There were British people in the audience and they gave me a tremendous welcome.

"I forgot the words of one song, but no one twigged and the club paid us £250."

Word quickly spread and Darren and his friends were invited to Les Caves des Rois, a swinging disco club at the exclusive Hotel Byblos in St Tropez.

Darren says: "On the first night, we were treated to about £400 worth of food, champagne and other drinks. They couldn't do enough. We went back another couple of times and were treated like superstars.

Meanwhile, Darren had met another French girl, ... He and three other ... members later left with her for her home in the central French town of Chateauroux.

..., 20, said at her home: "I met him in a bar and was convinced that it was Boy George." She said that she later learned his secret, but didn't let on.

She added: He and his friends stayed with me for four nights and I arranged an interview for him with a local radio station."

Darren says: "... test as interpreter. I was asked a lot of questions I didn't have answers for, but I got round them.

"The interviewer even asked me to appear on a TV show, but I thought that was too risky in case someone actually twigged that I wasn't Boy George.

Darren, who recently won a national newspaper as Boy George look-alike competition, says: "I'm often mistaken for him in Brighton, but France was unbelievable.

..., 20, another ... group member, says: "He was so convincing that even we called him George most of the time.

A third member ..., 20, says: "It all started as a giggle, but it got a bit out of hand in the end. We were worried that someone was going to discover the truth any minute."

A spokesman for Radio Berry Sud in Chateauroux confirmed that Darren had been interviewed as Boy George. And with several many people on the French Riviera were still unaware of the hoax. A spokesman for one hotel said: "Yes, Boy George was here. He was marvellous.

REALLY
GEORGE?

en is
f the
les

RROLL

ege! Or maybe
could easily be
s Peter.

m The winner of
mpetition to find
George lookalike.
ck the winner from
tries. And it was
he final three from
.. sure they are.

the ambition
y George,
cons a secondhand
tion, says: "I love
Boy George, but I'd
y own

is for
ht I've
spend
look-

not in
self by

Would you have spotted him,
folks? It's the real Boy George.

Darren Hogg ... "I was always a bit different from the other boys at school"

PICTURES BY BEVERLEY GOOD

it dif-
very
ge co-
asp.
in the
even
in the

nt so
got a
faceto-
secretly

a nasty.
if you
or I've
estime-

**And now
the best
of all**

As a rule people like Boy
George and they're very
nice to me.

■ **BUILDING WORKER**
Mark Goodwin reckons that
his Boy George image does
wonders when it comes to
pulling girls.

Mark, 18, of Whitstable,
Kent, says: "I first dressed
up as Boy George for a
fancy dress party.

"It was a real eye-opener
—the girls were all over me.
They love anyone who looks

The Gig's all set!

I lit my first cigarette of the day, I poked Randy in his side, to see if he was awake . . . . There was no response! I lay beneath a single cotton sheet, I looked at my body the white sheet emphasised the browness of my body, I was so brown, really brown . . . I liked my brown body. The song of the crickets echoed outside, it sounded as they were singing in unison. i got up and made my way downstairs to see if the others were about, but the villa was empty. There was nobody there? No one in the Garden?. It was completly silent and empty. I looked at the kitchen clock ticking away, it was gone noon. I must of needed my sleep, as I hadn't even heard Milly and Katy get up let alone go out. (Or maybe I was just knocked out last night from all the French Vino!)

"Randy, Randy" I shouted up the stairs, "Do you want a coffee?" . . . . I heard a grunt from upstairs "mmm". I made the coffee and called up to Randy to meet me in the garden and I would take them out there. I was shaking, I was scared and I felt really strange!! Did I have a hangover? Or did I have the DT's? Or was I getting a cold? I don't know . . . all I can remember was feeling really scared and weird!

Randy emerged from the bedroom and shufflled downstairs, through the kitchen and arrived in the garden as if he had sleepwalked. I gave him his coffee and a pair of sunglasses, he took them as if he was a robot. I told him not to squint as it would give him lines when he was older. He looked at me and I guess what he was saying in his head was . . . Oh shut up Daron!. "Lovely day" I said. "mmmmhhhmmmm" he grunted. "Shall we stay here today and tidy up the Villa and rehearse the words to the songs? I asked, he answered with another grunt.

"The girls must have got up early to do some shopping, and Annette and Bridgette had most probably gone to work in the market on their T-shirt stall? . . . do you think Randy?" "Mmmmhhhmmm" he grunted yet again. Randy wasn't very good in the mornings, he never said much anyway . . . but in the mornings it was 10 times worse, it wasn't his favourite time of day unless he was just coming in from a night on the tiles.

I suddenly remembered that we were meant to be going down the beach to meet up with Carol and Zoe. "Randy, shall we meet up with the girls or stay here and copy out the lyrics to the songs?" "Whatever!!!" He still wasn't awake . . . ! "I think Milly and Katy have already met up with them, so it won't matter" He just grunted . . . so totally UNINTERESTED!

We finished up our coffee, then cleaned the kitchen, made the beds, we were not your typical French maids . . . he he! Then we got ready, slapped on the suncream, grabbed a pile of paper, some pens, the cassette player, a glass each of wine and headed for the garden. We began to listen to the Culture club tape. It suddenly dawned on me, I did NOT know any of the words to the songs, it was just a line here and there. And the more we listened there were sentences we couldn't actually work out what Boy George was singing . . ." Sod this for a laugh "Randy suddenly blurted out "Let's go into town and see if we can see a copy of the Lp with a lyric sheet inside!" . . . "What a great idea

Randy" I replied . . . "Maybe we could get a photocopy of it?" he added. "Even better idea" I agreed . . . Me liked that idea . . . had not liked the thought of writing out loads of copies of each song . . . ! Randy always made our show tapes for the cabaret act back in England, so he knew all about the music we used and the covers and inside lyric sheets. I plonked the rasta hat and sunglasses (my disguise), left a note for the others telling them where we had gone incase they came back before us, and then Randy locked the door as we stepped out into the blazing sunshine. Off we strolled into the town centre of Ste Maxime, not a long walk at all I guess about 5-10 mins. AS we walked into the market we spied Bridgette and Annette. We asked them where the nearest record shop was?

"Just aroundz the corner" answered Annette. We told them we would catch up with them later. So around the corner we went and into the record shop. "Bonjour!" we said as we entered. "you ask" . . . "No you ask" we bickered between us. "Wotz do youz wantz to ask mez" the guy behind the counter asked. "Have you got Culture Clubs Lp?" Randy finally asked. "Mai wee, butz of courze I do" replied the Hippy looking record shop man. "Itz veryz popularz here in zee France", "Would it be possible for us to borrow the inner sleeve to photocopy the lyrics?" Randy asked. "Whyz of course!" replied the Hippy shopkeeper." I have a copyerz here I canz do it pour vous!, howz many cpoiez would vous likez?" . . . About 10 "I blurted out . . . . "Noz problemz for youz Boy George".

Oh Dear, he too thought I was really George, Bless him!" Well it was general knowledge around the town that Boy George/ Me was having a holiday here in Ste Maxime . . . and it was a pretty small town.

He returned 5 mins later, "Merci, How much do we owe you?" I asked, "For Youz, nothing" replied the Hippy record shop man. He then asked for my autograph, So I signed 2 copy's of the Culture Club Lp. He believed Randy was the bass player and asked him to sign the albums too. Randy frooze, he couldn't remember the bass players name?!!! "Are you ok . . . MIKEY?" I asked, he turned and grinned at me . . . . a sense of relief came over his face. We said our Goodbye's and thanked him once again, popped around to the French girls stall to give them 4 copies for the musicians. Bridgette said she would drop them off later on her way back to the villa. She also told us that she had a meeting with the club manager from The Saint to discuss and arrange the gig, "Don't forget we need at least 4 days to rehease "I added. "It probably wont bez until the weekendz" she answered. We said we would see them this evening, and waved them bye for now and set off for the beach to catch up with the rest of the girls.

Before long we were down at the beach near the bridge. All the girls were there relaxing upon the golden sand of the beach. We told them how we had managed to get copies of the lyrics. And told them that Bridgette was meeting the club manager. "It's very Risky" said Carol . . . not so sure in the light of day. "Oh! it's going to be FUN!" Milly retorted. Katy said nothing and Zoe just laughed her head off as usual. Randy and I decided to go back up to the villa to finish cleaning and grab a snack. We told Milly and Katy we would see them later, and to Carol and Zoe that we would have our first reheasal the next day. Then Milly asked about the musicians "when do we rehease with them?" "I don't really know yet Milly, I'm sure Bridgette will do that when she drops the lyrics off to them". Randy and I wandered up from the beach popping into the local supermarket to buy some sausages and potatoes for supper "Fancy Sausage and mash tonight Randy?". "MMmmmmmmmmmmmmm" he moaned salivating and smacking his lips.

Milly and Katy were the first back that evening, then Annette returned from the market and it was at least 2 hours before Bridgette arrived. Katy and Milly were busy in the kitchen cooking our good ol' fashioned English grub. When it was done, we all sat in the garden with more vino, and finally Bridgette told us the news . . . . I was desparate to hear it . . . and been trying to play it cool as if it was no big deal! "You all will be playing at The Saint next weekend, it's going to be advertised as The Allstars with guest Boy George from the group Culture Club." She went on to tell us we were getting £250 in English money. God I thought . . . that's alot of money (it was a great deal in the 80's). It was serious now, our first booking.

"We must all rehearse tomorrow," I said . . . . no turning back now!!!! I thought. We couldn't let anyone down. We thanked Bridgette for all her hard work in arranging it all. We sat chatting and drinking until it was time for bed.

As I layed in the shared bed with Randy, my mind ran riot. It was working overtime. I thought about Carol's worry from earlier.

Just say, all this is illegal?
Just say, if I get found out?
Would Boy George mind?
Would I get arrested?
What if I forgot the words?
Then suddenly I was in the land of Nod . . . dreaming. I was asleep. Drunk as usual!

The Rehearsal.

All the worries that echoed around my mind last night, were still there with the break of daylight. I awoke to that strange feeling I endured yesterday. I was still sweating terribly and shaking, I put it down to the amount of alcohol I was consuming during this holiday. But everyone else seemed to be fine, was it because I was only 15. At times it felt as if someone was bashing my head with a baseball bat side-ways. Maybe I had over done it. But I think deep inside I think I knew what was really bothering me subconsciously . . . . it was the idea of the up and coming show! It was a big thing. I really wasn't feeling myself at all. and to be honest I had, had enough and just wanted to go home to my Mum. And on the other hand I was excited beyond belief. It may sound strange today, but at the time was a very weird feeling and experience . . . truly something I really just can't explain.

I plodded down the stairs with my strange feeling body, holding on to the hand rail, to make some coffee, maybe that would help restore my balance. Randy was already there in the kitchen . . . something like a mirage as he was always dead to the world. The girls were in the garden . . . . not Annette or Bridgette as the were off selling their wares in the market. Milly said that she would go and collect Carol and Zoe at the bridge, to bring them back to our Villa to rehearse. We could have a little lunch and then get on with the hard slog of creating a show Boy George would be proud of! I actually really couldn't be bothered, but now I couldn't let everyone down, it was such a big deal now. And part of me still wanted to get out there and perform with all eyes upon me and do the show . . . . Get paid . . . and go HOME!

Then Randy rigged up the tape machine and speakers in the garden, ready for our rehearsal. There was not enough room to do it in the villa, and besides it's it was too darn hot! Randy put on the cassette, I was organising where we would be on the stage trying to envisage the whole look of it all. Katy popped out of the kitchen and said "let's wait to the others get here, and we have had lunch". Katy went back to cooking the lunch. I just wanted to be alone, go off and be all by myself. I still felt very strange. It was about another hour before Milly arrived with Zoe and Carol. They had been into the supermarket on the way to pick up some beer, wine, water and cola in case we got thirsty getting our act together. After we ate lunch we moved the table as it was in the way on our make shift stage area. Ok we were ready to Rock 'n Roll, let's get the show on the road! "I'm here", I said "you 2 there and you 3 there . . . !" I demanded . . . I was turning into Diva . . . he he. Zoe had got the giggles as usual, I turned and snapped at her "For God's sake Zoe, let's be serious . . . remember we are being paid for this, we have to be proffesional". For that slight moment I felt in control and quite grown up. I heard whispers from one of the girl's "Who does he think he is?" But I didn't care, it was all I could to do to focus on this rehearsal . . . I still wasn't feeling well and I was not in the mood to take any shit from anyone. I felt like saying "Look I'm the star here, they want me to perform—Not you". But I bit my tongue. well it was all of us really, but deep down I knew all the paying audience would want to see was Boy George. I know now it sounds abit star struck and bitter—but I was feeling a lot worse, really ill. I didn't let on but I think Milly had an inkling of some sort. I poured myself a large glass of wine, lit a cigarette and handed out the lyrics to the songs to everyone.

"How many songs are we doing then?" asked Milly. "About 8, the album I think? We will start with 'White Boy' and then end 'Do you really want to hurt me?'as it's the biggest hit, if they want more we can do 'Manshake', but we had done that with the one man band at the cafe bar, when we got there loads of times.

Randy pressed play, the machine began to whir and we began to sing along to the tape. I was doing loads of "oh's" and "woo's" and everyone else began filling in with the chorus and extra backing parts. Back in England we played this tape all the time as Culture Club were the biggest thing around and everyone seemed to have bought their first album. So we all knew it quite well. After about 5 songs we had a rest, and a chilled glass of beer. Carol said that Randy was tone-deaf and that he sounded vile. Zoe laughed, Milly said nothing, Katy just looked at her in disbelief and I just didn't respond. Randy got up and walked off in a huff into the kitchen.

I wasn't suprised at all, we had been living inside each others pockets now for weeks, everything was getting tense, fragile and a little touchy between us all. Then adding the pressure of this gig. When coming on holiday, we had no idea that this whole Boy George thingy was going to happen and it was now a massive strain on the group. It was affecting us all in differing ways. Here we were rehearsing in the hot sun for a show not having fun in the sun, I bet the others thought why on earth did he bring his Boy George clobber? But I did, I'm 15 and do things like that . . . . It was too late now and that was that!

We carried on without Randy, I was upset by this because I wanted Randy to be part of the stage show. But when Randy is pissed off . . . RANDY IS PISSED OFF! Big Time!

Katy joined him in the kitchen and prepared some more food, we all sat around the re-postioned table to eat. Randy said that he wasn't bothered if he didn't come on stage anyway. But I made a point saying that Randy still would get paid, he had already been working on the show with me doing lyrics and setting up the sound etc for our rehearsals. With the 4 musicians there was 10 of us, so we all would get £25 each, not too bad for 1983. I know Bridgette didn't want paying, she had asked us to all wear her t-shirts on stage to publicize her t-shirt company.

"Mines dirty!" said Katy "And mine" said Milly . . . . I'm sure Bridgette will give us new ones to wear for the show to wear on stage" I responded. Zoe and Carol said they had to leave because there was a free barbeque at the camp site. And time was moving on, we had been reheasing for about 6 hours. Oh doesn't time fly when you are having fun . . . NOT! It was still hot and sunny and I felt exhusted, everyone was kind of tired . . . . We sent Carol and Zoe in the right direction back to town.

Katy was clearing up after the nibbles, Randy was putting the stereo back in the villa. I sat with Milly and chatted and chatted, we must of talked for ages as all of a sudden the French girls were back . . . we heard the car pull up. They joined us in the garden. They were starring at me in a most peculiar way? I asked what was wrong? "You look so different, without your make—up and hat on!" Annette said still really looking deeply at me. "OH SHIT!" I thought

Daron Hogg

They knew my secret . . . I'd forgotten to put on my Boy George disguise . . . . I think that Annette and Bridgette guessed at that moment I was not the real McCoy . . . But they never let on . . . .

Viva St Tropez.

It was yet another boiling hot, sticky and sunny day. Bridgette decided to take the day off from her T-shirt stall and asked me if I would like to join her for an afternoon in St Tropez.

"I'd love to" I replied to her. She told me that now that the show was booked it might be a good idea to walk the roads around St Tropez to do some self publicity. But to be honest I didn't really fancy walking around St Tropez fully made up, smiling at one and all, signing autographs and begging the rich holiday makers to come and see my show at the weekend. Everyone else seemed well up for it, and as I had never been to St Tropez . . . what the hell!! I'd go.

Randy, katy, Milly and I went up to the bedrooms to get dressed up. I wore a white turban thingy on my head, a little a bit of make up, very large sunglasses, a huge Viv Westwood shirt and some really baggy oversized white dungarees and leather flip flops. (I know now it sounds mad and a little bit weird), but it was 1983 and that was my kind of bizarre fashion at the time. I was dressed to impress as Boy George (in disguise). Randy had crimped his dreadlocks and went topless, and like me huge dungarees, Milly wore a cut off/cropped T-shirt with pedal pushers and very high heels . . . a black pair of 6" stilleto's . . . . and Katy wore ripped denim jeans and a boob tube and rags tied into her hair . . . We looked good, Ok maybe a little strange . . .

But we would not be missed put it that way! We looked like 80's English Popstars, and that was the idea!

Bridgette said it might be a good idea if we all popped into the club @The Saint@ to pick up some leaflets from the manager, that were advertising our show on Saturday and hand them out while we wandered around St Tropez.

So we were ready, we all piled into the rusty old citroen, this time with the roof down. The music was as loud as it possibly could be in the old hired car and made our way. We were St Tropez bound. I wondered out loud if anyone thought that Zoe and Carol were at the beach today. But Milly told me that they were moving tents as there's had been near flooding on the camp site. But not to worry about them, they'd be fine and we would catch up later with them . . . or tomorrow.

Our first stop was 5 minutes down the road, stopping at the club in Ste Maxime, we pulled up and parked outside 'The Saint'. The manager saw us arrive and waved, "Come up to ze terrace and havez a drinkz" he called. So we tumbled out of the rusty hire car and joined him on the terrace.

"Champagnez for de Boy George and Friendz" he said to his waiter. We all sat around the table overlooking the French Meditearean. People were coming up and asking for my autograph—which I gladly obliged. I had run out of cigarettes, so I asked the manager if I could have one of his. "of courze for tu anythingz" he clicked his fingers and his waiter returned he spoke to him very fast in French, and within a few minutes he returned with 3 packets just for me. I hastily stuck them in my bum bag. "Merci" I said "Merci, beaucoup".

He showed us the leaflets, they looked the Biz, very professional and appealing. He then showed us the local daily paper with an advert advertising the Saturday show.

They price to get in was about £10 . . . which was a hell of a lot for those days, I hope I could pull it off, I was getting a little nervous about it. But another bottle of champagne arrived the third in half an hour. It was getting on it was past 3pm and I was feeling slightly tipsy. Bridgette didn't drink as she was driving us all to St Tropez and stuck to orange juice. "More Champagnez???" asked the manager. "Oh weeeee" I squeeled in my giggly state. So we downed a 4th bottle. Bridgette then told us it was time to make a move and get ourselves to St Tropez. So with the leaflets we thanked the manager for his hospitality and piled back into old rusty and set off for St Tropez. Music blared out as the breeze blew through our hair. On the tape machine I remember the Marianne Faithful track playing called Broken English, a theme of many of our days there in France. To this very day every time I hear that track I am transported back to that summer.

Before long we arrived in St Tropez and headed toward the bar in the harbour in an attempt to attract attention. Bridgette ordered an orange juice for herself and a bottle of wine for us. We sat at a table, the previous customers had left a tip and i slid the francs to the edge of the table and into my hand and straight into my bum bag. Within 5 minutes people were coming up to me to ask for autographs and have their photograph taken with me. (I would dearly love to see those photos now!) Bridgette suggested that we made a tour of the posh boutiques to see if they would have our leaflets by their cash desks. Also to see if we could blag some designer togs to wear for the gig that would help publicise their shop? I was drunk by now, and laughed "Ole" . . . must of thought I'd gone to Spain . . . ! Firstly we popped into Chanel where they gave me a T-shirt for free, then on to the next where I got a pair of shoes. And next another designer shop who I cant mention gave me a naff handbag. I really dont know what they thought I would do with one of their handbags on stage? Maybe dance round it?? Or sing "Do you really want to hurt me?" and hit the drummer with it! But who cares it was free and it would be something I could give to my Mum on my return to the UK.

It was getting quite late, I was hot, bothered and feeling very knackered, so we headed off back to Saint Maxime and the villa. It had been a nice day in St Tropez, I just wished that I had been able to relax and enjoy it, but I was feeling tense about the gig. But I was now having to dart up alleyways and hiding in shops to avoid photographers, The Paparazzi . . . Oh well that's being famous for you!

The Day Before.

It was now Friday. The day before the show. Bridgette woke me up that morning to tell me that she had arranged for us to meet up with the session musicians and to do a last minute rehearsal at the club—The Saint. She said that it would be at 6pm. And the manager had laid on drinks and a buffet for us all. Everything was twisting in my brain, I didn't know all the lyrics to the songs! How many tickets had they sold? Would I pull this off?

Bridgette answered the phone, the ticket sales were going Fantasico . . . They were very nearly sold out. It was going to be a very packed house. There were going to be photographers, the local newspaper and also the local TV station. My God I was more than concerned now I was bloody frightened. I told the others the good news, while inside I had more than a case of Butterflies.

We had to meet up with Carol and Zoe to let them know the schedule, and mostly what we were up against in this show, it had gone so much bigger than we ever thought. So we strolled down to the beach to catch up with the other two. Thank goodness they were there as usual when we arrived. I told them not to forget their photocopied lyric sheets and to be at the club at 6pm, It was the only real reheasal with the band and we only had 4 hours at that to get it right. "6 o'clock on the dot . . . pleeeeeaaasssse, don't be late!" I said to them. Everything was set up now.

Milly, Randy. Katy and I went back to the villa to beautify ourselves for the 6pm rehearsal. We grabbed a bite to eat which we ate in the garden. Two drinks later it was 5.40pm and time to head toward the club. Once again we piled into old rusty and made our way there.

"Bonjour!" said the club manager. "Everyone is here!" I was really suprised that Carol and Zoe were there on time. Miracles can happen. They—Bridgette and Annette came back about 7pm. I thought it was really sweet of them to shut their t-shirt stall early to be there at the club with us. were not the worlds greatest time keepers, so I was extremely happy to see them there. The band had already set up all their equipment on the stage. It was luckily quite a big stage considering that there would be 10 of us on stage. The band plugged everything in. I was bossing everyone about and pointing you go there, I'll be here, you two there, etc. Then when the band started I was them commenting that's too fast or slow! Poor Randy just sat and watched us all on stage because of Carol saying to him the week before that he was tone deaf and couldn't sing. I don't think he really minded and after all he was still getting a cut in the performing fee for the show. I found it a bit sad, because I really wanted Randy to be up there on the stage with us.

The songs were going very well, the band had already rehearsed, they were note perfect. But the thing that shocked me was suprisingly enough my friends had leant and actually remembered all the words to the Culture Club songs! We ran through the 8 songs we had prepared. And then thought we best do Manshake in case we went so well and needed to do an encore. (I thought to myself I'm sure that the audience would want us too). It had taken us about 3 hours and we had gone through all the songs 3 times. It sounded wonderful having a live band instead of practising to a tape machine. They were brillant, they usually were session musicians for a famous French singer. We were so lucky. The band put all there musical instruments in a huge locked dressing room, as tonight was a normal night at the Nightclub. And they didn't want anyone walking off with any of their equipment. My microphone kept giving feedback, but the DJ from the club said he'd make sure it was sorted by tomorrow's gig. We were all in OUR dressing room which was over looking the harbour, There was champagne, wine, food . . . Everything! I lit up my cigarette, poured myself a glass of champagne and made a toast "Good Luck to us all for the show!". We sat around and chatted for about an hour, we finished all the booze and buffet. We arranged to be at the club again at 6pm to have one more practise before the actual show. We were due onstage at 11pm, the doors opened at 8pm, it was a mix of a disco and live band night!

We thanked the manager for the drinks and buffet, said Goodbye to everyone in the club and we all left to go back to the villa. The band and Carol and Zoe . There we had late night drinks and talked until the early hours of the morning. I think that the band had worked out that I wasn't really the real mc coy of Boy George. I don't think they really even care to be honest, it was still a laugh and joke. As we sat in the cool of the night in the garden, moths fluttered around the candles. Bridgette then pulled out some of her T-shirts from her bag and asked us to wear them for the show. I wasn't too sure that it was really Boy George, But I took the top just the same. I still wanted one and had an idea of what I could do with it. It was a very good idea. (I'll let you know later.)

The band went home and Zoe and Carol made their way to the campsite. We finalised our plans, 6pm at the club. It was nearly time for one more reheasal and 'The Big Gig'. I was getting so nervous now, in just 24 hours I was really going to have to pretend I was Boy George and star in this show in the south of France. It was going to be mad! Time for bed!!!

The Show—My Madness, My Brain.

I awoke very early that Saturday morning with so much going through my brain, my mind was on fire about the show that night. Was I getting stressed out? I thought I had better take it easy or I would lose the plot before evening arrived. I went out into the villa's garden clutching a mug of coffee. I really must not drink any alcohol during the day and should probably cut down on the cigarettes or my voice would be awful that night. The two french girls had left already to do their stall. It was the last day of doing so. The rest of my friends were still fast asleep. On Tuesday Bridgette was heading home back to Paris, and Annette was going back to her home in the town of Charteroux on the Wednesday. The season was now drawing to a close. It would soon be time for us all to do the same . . . back to good old B llighty.

I wandered back into the kitchen, I was more awake after my cup of coffee and noticed that Annette had left us all a note on the table. I picked it up and read the message. They would be back at 3pm, they were only going half a day today. As it was half day closing at the market. I was guessing they were far more excited than they were letting on. I poured myself another coffee, lit my first cigerette of the day and enjoyed the morning sunshine once more. it was a beautiful day yet again. I found it hard to believe that i had been here for 4 weeks already. I sat there puffing on my cigarette, sipping my coffee running the film of my life in Ste Maxime, remembering everything I had been through in such a short amount of time . . . The motorway and losing Zoe, the doughnuts, sleeping under the bridge, the fat balding man, and The Angel that had saved me from my hideous ordeal. Tears ran down my cheeks, i started to cry, really sob barely being able to breathe. What the hell would I tell people and my Mum what had happened to me in France in that amount of time. I was replaying the whole thing through my minds eye and began to really worry about what could of happened, the tradegy that could of befallen me. Thinking 'What if . . . Just if . . . ?' I began to feel very strange again, like I had done for days now. I began to wonder if I was on the verge of a nervous breakdown? Looking back now, I think it must of been extremely traumatic for a 15 year old boy. All I wanted to do now was the show tonight and then get home safely to my Mum in England.

Gradualy the others woke up and made their way to sit with me in the garden. Katy looked at me, she could see I had been crying and came across and embraced me in her arms. I think she too was very nervous about the show that night. But she didn't realise that actually it wasn't that, that had caused the tears. It was the reminising of the previous 4 weeks. We all sat there enjoying the sun, chatting for ages. Milly said that after the show we must make descions on when we were making our way back to England. And more to the point, who was traveling with who . . . I thought to myself I don't really want to go back with Zoe . . . she might desert me again! How we were to return to dieppe had not really crossed my mind, I didn't really want to hitchhike again, the idea of being on the motorway again . . . and what if all that nasty shit happened again . . . I really didn't want to think about it. Milly rushing her words as normal suggested that it might be a better idea if I travel with Randy, two boys together (phew I felt so relieved with that idea, I'd be so much happier being with Randy). Milly said she would travel back with Katy . . . and as Zoe and Carol seemed to have spent so much time together it was obvious they would want to be together. I'm sure that Zoe would be happy about it too, I'm sure she really didn't want to be with me.

The afternoon dragged by so slowly, we were all in the bathroom at one point deciding on the outfit we would each wear for the show . . . It was like the aftermarth of a fashion show in the bedroom, the contents of everyone's rucksacks were strewn on every surface. Milly and Katy decided that they would wear the t-shirts Bridgette had given them(but they had cut them to be crop tops showing their midriffs) with their white dungerees!

I put on my really baggy white dungerees with an extra large Viv Westwood shirt. "What about Bridgette's t-shirt, aren't you wearing that?" Milly asked in a questioning manner. "You better wear it!". I had an idea as I knew I had to wear it. But Bridgette had not said how . . . now had she? I had decided to to cut up the t-shirt into long stripes and tie them into my hair, it was a very 80's think to do and of course Boy George had done it many times. And if she said anything I was still wearing it, wasn't I? Milly handed me her old dirty one to cut up, which I thought so sweet as I still got to keep mine. I cut it up to make a punky bum flap, which I attached with safety pins. I asked Katy to help me braid my hair with the t-shirt rags, which she did. Carol would be doing my make-up that night, she was so good at it. We put our show outfits in plastic bags . . .

How glamarous? And all was ready, so back to the garden, a glassof vino in hand to await Bridgette and Annette.

At about 3pm we heard the car pull up and the french girls were back and joined us in the garden. I could see Bridgette was starring at my hair from the corner of my eye. Then she spoke" Iz that one of my t-shirts?" I said it was and she seemed pleased that I was wearing her t-shirt in some way, whatever it maybe or no matter what it looked like! We had another glass and got our show stuff together, it was time to head toward The Saint Nightclub for our last rehearsal and the big night ahead . . . . THE SHOW!!!

Carol and Zoe were already there when we arrived along with the four musicians. We dumped our show gear in the dressing room and made our way to the stage to begin our final rehearsal. There was no turning back now! It all went so quickly, time flew by. We had a few hiccups, a few up's and down's, forgetting the odd lyric in a couple of songs and Zoe bursting into fits of giggles . . . but basically it was there.

We went upstairs to our dressing room, where again the club manager had laid on a lovely buffet for us, and of course more bottles of wine and champagne, as well as beer. I glanced out of the window the sun glisterning on the meditiranean . . . I had a strange sense of calm and fear all rolled into one, anxious as time ticked by. "Half hour til ze show" came a voice from behind the dressing room.

"Well this is it guys!" I said. Carol put the finishing touches to my make up, which looked absolutly amazing, we were dressed and ready to Rock 'n Roll. Carol's outfit for the night was one of my World's End Viv Westwood shirts, with leggings and big boots, while Zoe wore another of Bridgette's t-shirts and ripped jeans and 6" high heels. The band all wore Bridgette's t-shirts with jeans. Shame she had done her last day at the market, I'm sure she would have sold loads tomorrow! We looked very professional all matching, but not in a uniform way though! I could hear the audience from the dressing room. It made me feel uneasy. It was packed to the hilt. "15 minutes until the show" came the voice from behind the door again. I lit my cigarette, and took a long drag. I had butterflies now, but large tropical ones not your cabbage whites! I glupped down another of cold wine . . . and then powdered my nose!

"Are we all ready?" asked Milly. "Yes" we replied with energy and fear! "As soon as they introduce us the band goes on first, then us four and then Daron!" "Who's Daron?" I asked trying not to give the game away. "Oh, sorry, I mean George!" She quickly replied. "Right, all set then?" I looked around the room . . . . It was the moment . . . "It's now or never!" The annonncement echoed along the corridor to the stage, first in French and then in English . . . .

"Please welcome The Allstars with special guest Boy George from Culture Club". The audience roared, cheered and clapped. On went the band, the beat of the drums pulsated then on went the four girls, . . . then it was ME!!! Randy stood there watching in the wings! . . . The tune began . . . we were starting with the song White Boy. and we were on and performing . . . it went down REALLY well. The audience loved US! There were flash bulbs going off everywhere from the crowds cameras. There was even a TV crew there, they were all lapping it up . . . . They thought I was Boy George! I was in my element, but by the fifth song I was fluffing up my lyrics, I couldn't remember the words. But by this stage I didn't care and made up anything that sounded vaguely like what it should be. We even got our encore of Manshake. And the audience wanted even more . . . But my voice was begining to crack by this point, after all I wasn't a professional singer, and at 15 my voice was still breaking and finding its manly balance. It had gone so well, we waved to the crowd as we exited the stage. The disco music began bellowing out of the speakers and from the DJ booth the DJ thanked us . . . And that was that.

Looking back now, it had happened so quickly and was very much a blur as it happened. Back in the dressing room, I lit up again, thanked everyone, opened a bottle of champagne. I felt so strange. I was having a Greta Garbo moment, I wanted to be alone. I took myself off to the toilet in the corner of the dressing room. I locked the door behind me, pushed down the seat and collasped on to it and burst into tears. I cried my eyes out, I sobbed. And all Carol's beautiful make up job became sumdged around my eyes. I looked like a wet faced panda. I was shaking, and sweated. I wanted to escape out of the window, be totally alone, jump on the next flight to England. I was having some kind of breakdown. I felt Vile!. Empty and alone, rejected and unwanted. After all no one had come to see me Daron. They came to see Boy George . . . and I wasn't him. Was this the reason I felt so strange? Pretending to be someone I was not?

After a while I came out. We were paid and finished of the buffet, well I picked at it, my tummy was all mixed up with my confused emotions. The rest of the gang knew I was upset, but didn't really understand why? The door to the dressing room opened and a man from another club 'Byblos' in St Tropez came in and asked me if I would play his club next week, he said he would pay £1000.00. I declined, I said "No". I had, had enough, I just wanted to go HOME. He seemed fine about it and asked us to be his guests at his club the next evening. We said we would try, but no promises. He said everything would be on the house, we could have what ever we liked . . . . I thought to myself "Ooh God, NOT again!" I just wanna go home. Sod the money. Sod France . . . I was so over it all!

Zoe and Carol go Home.

There was a knock at the door very early the next morning, it must of been around 8am, who on earth was up before God at this hour? We were still fast asleep in the land of dreams. Bridgette got up and answered the door . . . it was Zoe and Carol. They had come round to let us know that the had made the descion to go back to England, to go home today. They said that they felt it was time to go even though they had a most brillant time. Fab! They had just enough money to get to Dieppe and the ferry back. It was all air kisses Good Bye . . . we were being so theatrical darling! We hugged and told them to take care and be very careful going back . . . memories of the hideous journey down flashed through my mind . . . Where I had lost Zoe? Don't go there Daron. I thought to myself. And that we would call them when we got home. "It would be probably the end of the week" added Annette. I looked across at her with a puzzled look "Why the end of the week?" I asked. "Because I was going to ask you if you would like to come and stay with me in Chateroux breaking your journey home" she answered. "We will have to think about it!" Milly told her.

We waved Zoe and Carol Good Bye . . . that was it they were off home. It was kind of sad to see them go as it meant the summer holiday was slowly creeping to an end. And I guess we really did need to get back to England.

Bridgette said that we all should go to Saint Tropez tonight to have a last party night together. The villa was booked up until Wednesday morning, but Bridgette's flight was on Tuesday. So Annette would have to drop off the keys to the owner on Mercrodi matin . . . . oh I'm going all French for a moment. And then it would be time to start the hitchhiking once again. So a last time 'Good Bye Party' would be the perfect ending to our fabulous French adventure. I started to feel a lot better and not at all like it was the last week. I was so up for it. We would not have to worry about money in Saint Tropez as it was FREE! The owner had invited us and so it was on him!!! So yes . . . Let's Party like it's 1999! We all agreed . . . woo hoo! Now on to important things . . . like what were we going to wear that night! "Let's really go for it" I said . . . with a really wicked glint in my eye. I was so looking forward to it now!

I now wanted to let Bridgette and Annette know the truth of my true identity.

So I opened my mouth and blurted it out . . . ." You know I'm not really Boy George!!!!". They looked at me and smiled. "We know" they said together. "we have known all along, but we thought as you had kept up the pretence so long we didn't want to spoil your dream of being him for this time". We fell about laughing in the kitchen until our sides ached. It was such a relief to be me again at last . . . . no more running upstairs to throw my Rasta George hat on anymore . . . Phew! I told them my real name was Daron. They said that they knew that too . . . it seems the joke was really on me! I said that I hadn't said anything because I thought that they would throw us out of the villa. "Oh Daron don't be silly we would of never have done that to you!" Bridgette responded . . . "Annette and I have really enjoyed your company and hope we will stay touch always".

We had an early supper and then all took turns to use the shower. I walked down to the telephone box and phoned my Mum. I told her all the tales of what had gone on as quickly as I could and that I should be home maybe by the end of the week. I think she was a little more than happy to hear my voice and to know that I had been having a lovely time from me and not just on postcards. I said we were leaving Ste Maxime on Wednesday morning and should be in Chateroux by evening and that we were going to stay with Annette for a day or 2 before starting onwards to Dieppe . . . and then back home to her. I told her I loved her and put the receiver down, It was so good to talk to my Mum and hear her voice . . . even though I had fun I missed her.

"Ready yet?" someone shouted "Nearly!!!" I answered. We all looked bloody fantastic, dressed to the nines . . . and for the last time here in France I had to be George. We looked great as normal lipstick, powder, hair done . . . ! And the waft of scent on everyone was Bridgettes perfume that we had all borrowed, so if they didn't see us coming they would definitely smell us! We all folded ourselves into the rusty old citreon and off we set for the party . . . Watch out Saint Tropez here we come! It was quite amazing that we all 6 of us actually fitted into the car but we did. The 3 girls in the back, Bridgette driving and Randy and me sitting up front with her. Randy's head would of been hitting the roof, luckily it was off as he was pearched on my lap. The music blarring out which we sang along too. I asked Bridgette about the session musicians. "Were they going to be there tonight?" "Weee, yes of course George . . . I mean

Daron" . . . she laughed. "They will meet us at the Disco Byblos".

I thought . . . Oh good, It would be great to say a proper Good Bye to them as they were part of our holiday and adventure . . . . Oh! Poor Saint Tropez, we were going to paint the town red tonight . . . . !

The Party in St Tropez.

It was early evening when we pulled up into St Tropez, the place was buzzing, a very holiday atmosphere. The holiday makers were everyway you turned. Sitting in the bars. Down by the harbour it was the locals and the rich French Riviera set drinking their champagne on their yachts. We parked good ol' Rusty the car along the quay of the harbour. We poured out onto the pavement. Bridgette suggested that we should have a quick drink before making our way to the club. We plonked ourselves down outside the first bar we came upon. We ordered some wine, what a surprise!

I lit up a cigarette and within moments YET another crowd had gathered and were asking for autographs and photos. Boy was I sick of being The Boy! But never the less I obliged. By this point I was beyond caring what anyone said or thought. I was just going through the motions. NUMB! It was the last few days and very nearly time to leave the cote du azure and GO back to Blighty.

We finished up the bottle of wine, I paid, I was even beyond working out how much each of us should contribute. It was about £12 not cheap, but it was St Tropez. We meandered up to the club/ hotel Byblo's and introduced ourselves to the doorman, who happily let us enter and said he would let the manager know of our arrival. We found a table on the edge of the dance floor and parked ourselves down. A waiter arrived and took our order. I told him that the manager had said it was all on the house for our party. He went off and checked, and returned about five minutes later and said "Ah Oui, everything is the compliments of ze manager!" So we settled for champagne. Well, I was here at his request being George. We also ordered more wine and some orange juice. The drinks arrived with the four sessions musicians right behind them. We greeted the boys, glasses clinked as we toasted one another. We chatted, they were really sweet French guys we talked about life in general nothing deep and meaningful.

They were staying at some French singer's villa, (whom I now know as a friend all these years later via Facebook).

It was great to finally get a chance to talk with them, I think I was far too stressed before the show. They told me all about their tour that was coming up and their music. It was so nice to talk properly in a relaxed manner. The waiter came by and left more bottles of Champagne and wine on our tables. Annette asked where the manager was and the waiter told us he would join us very soon. "Do youz want anythinz Boyz George?" he asked me. "Yes please" I replied. I ordered more cigs and a cheese roll I was starving. How glamerous is that? A cheese roll! The others were taken a back and started going on that they couldn't believe that I had ordered cigarettes and a cheese roll!. Well had the manager not said we could have anything we wanted. Sod I wanted a Bloody Cheese roll . . . Big Deal!

Photographers were snapping away and yet more drink arrived, and yes we drank it. The Manager finally came across he had been busy dealing with work before he could join us. We shook hands. Again he asked me if we would do a show for him the following week for a £1,000, I polietly refused once again and made up some story of I had things scheduled back in England next week. It sounds mad now turning down all that money considering how much that was back then. But I was so over living in disguise, another week of it would of sent me over the edge. England was calling me loud and clear. I wanted to go HOME! Little did he know we had to hitch the length of France to do so. I was glad that I had said yes to cutting the journey by staying with Annette. That would be nice. The Manager was so very kind and sweet he must of spent a grand on us that night . . . all for nothing. But he thought he had a famous popstar in his club that night . . . so he was happy. Maybe he had thought I would change my mind when drunk . . . Like that was going to happen? No, I had made up my mind!

We had a Fantastic time there that night at The Disco Byblos, but then who wouldn't off had . . . . It was FREE! It was getting quite late and I was begining to feel the strain and really tired. Word had got around we were there and we were asked by other club owners to come and join them in their various clubs. I didn't want to go. I wanted to go back to the villa, wash my face of all the slap and get this wig and hat off. I refused at did a dramatic yawn. I really, really needed a good nights sleep. I had to make some excuse didn't I? I was so drunk by now. Mily and Katy decided to go on to another Bar? club or whatever. I was beyond caring now. They left with the session musicians and disappeared into the night.

I told Bridgette I was tired and would love to go back to the villa. So we did, me Randy Annette and Bridgette in the car, it had been a wonderful night, but the whole saga of a false identity, the show and my constant drinking . . . I wanted my bed and slllleeeeeepppp!!!

We arrived back at the villa and chilled in the garden with yet more wine then I dragged my knacked body to my bed. I slept like a log, but at about 5 o'clock I was woken by Milly and Katy returning from their jaunt to other clubs in St Tropez. They came bouncing in to Randy and me, they had, had a brillant time, but mainly to break some unexpected news that Milly had enough money for us all to get the train back to Chateroux with Annette on Wednesday. I asked her in my bleery eyed state, how she had got the money to do that! "Don't you worry your little head about that!" she answered patting me on the head. "I've got the money and we are going by train, end of story, it's the least I can do after your nightmare of a journey you had getting down here! And remember Daron I was meant to look after you.!". She said that she would go down to the train station later in the day when she got up and buy and book the fares for Wednesday. I must admit I was so dozey, still tired and half asleep I wasn't really taking it in. I don't think Randy was either, it seemed like a part of a dream. As I wouldn't have to hitch for part of the way . . . how wonderful was that! As I drifted of back to sleep I remember thinking again . . . how on earth had she got the money? Until this very day I have no idea how she managed to get the cash. Maybe she found it? or had done what I did, stealing it from tables . . . the tips! Whatever it was Milly had come to our rescue.!!! We were going by train . . . *zzzzzzzzzzzzzzzzzzzzzzzzzzzzz*!

Au Revoir St Maxime!
Bonjour Chateroux!

Bridgette was up at the crack of dawn, gathering up and packing all her belongings ready for her flight back to Paris. It was a sad affair 'Our Holiday' was coming to an end. Everyone met up in the kitchen downstairs and had coffee and croissants for breakfast. It was yet another glorious day, very hot, so we relocated outside in the garden for our last breaky all together. It was a very long chat with Bridgette about our last 5 weeks of our summer holiday in the south of France. It had at times been tearful, other times wonderful fun, but above all it had been a great adventure that we had all shared together. Bridgette delved into her handbag and pulled out her business cards and handed them around to us all. "Pleaze keep in touch wont you?" she said her voice a little cracking. I think she was sad to leave us. (We did keep in touch for a couple of years after the French Adventure.) All her bags were packed, her Taxi ordered it was time for her to depart to the airport in Nice. We stood around in a semi circle and all kissed and hugged and finally waved her Goodbye as the taxi exited from the villa. We were disappearing Carol and Zoe . . . gone already, now Bridgette. And then there were Five! Sounds like an Enid Blyton book. Five go exploring in France. I was kind of hankering to get home though too.

Today was clean the villa day! Annette organised a final evening supper for us all! It would have to be a bedtime of a reasonable hour as we were to catch the train pretty early for us night owls.

Milly and Katy went into town up to the station to get the train tickets for tomorrow. Randy, Annette and me started the clean up of the villa. After an hour or so Annettte went into town to get supplies for the last supper in villa. We didn't take too long clearing the villa up, thank goodness. But then we had been pretty house proud and cleaned every few days. We had not lived like sluts . . . we had been Annette and Bridgette's guests it was the least we could do.

The girls came back from the town. And seemed so shocked to see that Randy and I had finished the cleaning. We had cleaned the villa from top to bottom. On her way back Annette had dropped off the old rusty Citreon to the hire firm. That really kind of finalised we were moving on again. She said that she would drop off the keys to the villa to the owner on our way to the train station the next morning. We were booked for the 10.30am train, so needed to leave about 9.30am at the very latest.

The evening whizzed by, we had a lovely supper of pasta and vino, cleared up the plates etc and then packed our bags ready for the off in the morning. I remember we all went to bed really early that night, partly because it was the excitement of going home. Well Chateroux! And it was only 125 miles from Dieppe so the thought of only a little bit of hitch hiking was not so much of a worry to me in the slightest! Morning seemed to arrive quickly. I grabbed a quick shower, a quick coffee and we all went around the villa closing the windows and fastening the shutters. Passports??? Yes! Money? Yes etc . . . etc! We were off!

The Train station was probably actually only 10 minutes from the villa, so we arrived in time to have another coffee and a cigarette. We found a carriage and plonked ourselves down. We watched all the beautiful countryside hurry pass. I felt a bit sad, after all that I had been through I was now leaving the South of France. "Maybez next year" Annette piped up . . . It was like telepathy . . . could she read my mind? "Yeah maybe next year?" I agreed. Many towns and villages flew by, some of which bought the memories of my journey down. I shuddered. The constant sound of the train must of lulled me to sleep as I awoke a couple of times with a start. It was a long journey.

"We arez herez" said Annette waking me up! We jumped off the train grabbing hold of our bags. The weather was just the same as from where we had left. Hot and Sticky. "Welcome to Chateroux" Annette proclaimed with vigour. "I only live a couplez of streets away from here".

The town was very laid back and small, lovely old houses and of course the obligotory Market Square, the little quaint little shops and cafes everywhere. We arrived at Annette's abode, she lived on the 2nd floor of the house. NO lift, so we had to make our way up the old wooden staircase. We got inside . . . It was wonderful, 3 massive rooms, tiled floors and a balcony overlooking the main cobbled street below. The sleeping arrangements were that Randy and I would share one of them put me up beds and the girls were to share with Annette. It was so kind of her to let us stay for a few days. We gathered to gether the last of our francs to get food. I asked Milly what we were going to do about the Ferry fares? She said that she would give our group manager Jimmy Jones a call and ask him to get some tickets for us to be picked up at Dieppe. She told me not to worry . . . so I didn't! It's not like I was going to be stuck in France for the rest of my life was it?

Annette was really sweet that night, she took all of us out for pizza, as she decided after all she couldn't be bothered to cook! And of course when she came to England in the future we could repay the favour of all she had done for us.

I went out as me at long last . . . Just simple plain old Daron. I didn't crave the attention anymore. I wanted to be me! Was I Daron anymore??? It was a lovely meal, the wine even better it was all very French but Italian too. A couple of guys that knew Annette came over to our table to chat with her. She introduced us . . . me as me!!! They said they worked for a local radio station, and before I realised what I was saying the words came flowing from my lips . . . "Oh you should have Boy George as your special Guest" . . . what the hell was I saying? WE told them he was back at Annette's resting, we would ask him if he'd join them for their show tommorrow.

Once they were out of ear shot, Milly turned to me . . . "Oh God, Daron . . . NOT again!!! "Why not? It's not going to hurt now is it? I looked at the bussiness card they had left me . . . I'd ring them as George in the morning.

Radio Berry Sud in Chateroux.

The next morning was yet another totally gorgeous day, we were so used to it, it was normal now! All the blag I told the 2 men from the radio station had hit it's toll. "What do you think Annette?" I asked "Is it a a good idea?". She told me how I would even be paid for the interview so I thought what the hell, let's do it. Then I asked "How much?". Well we were broke so any amount would be rather good right now! "Oh about 500 Francs", she replied . . . that was about £50 in those days!!! "Ok I'll do it!". I asked Randy to come to be my support, I was still feeling vunerable about my true identity of who I was these days. Randy of course agreed, so Annette called the radio station and arranged the time etc with the men who worked there. Annette was going to act as interpreter. It was arranged for 6pm that evening. And the fee was just as she had said—500 Francs. Katy and Milly said they would listen to the interview in the apartment.

At this time—Everything was so out of hand, so what did I have to lose? Nothing! And I'd we would have 500 francs to help us with the return to England. We . . . that's me and Randy got ourselves ready starting at 3.30pm. Of course drinking wine and smoking about 50 fags while putting on the Boy George Slap YET again. I did it the best I could but I really wished Carol had been there to do it! I was a bit of an amatuer when it came to make up. Thinking of Carol I wondered if she and Zoe had got home safely. Of course they would be . . . after all they were pretty girls and would of got a lift in no time at all.

Randy, Annette and Boy George/ me all walked along the little French streets of Chateroux to the local radio station. Everyone we passed took photo's of me, asking for autographs . . . I really dont thing this little town in France knew what was going on!! Annette was telling them to go home and listen to the radio at 6pm. Bless her!. She really didn't have to do all of this. BUT she was our friend now, and I dont think she really minded. I think it was quite exciting for her. After all being a small town girl, Chateroux was a bit boring for her. We arrived at the radio station at 5.30pm, half an hour to go. The Green Room person came to my rescue with the cigarettes and wine. I was kind of tipsy and I think Randy and Annette were too. I had to sign something . . . . I wondered WHAT IF they ever found out I wasn't George!? They handed me an envelope containing the 500 Francs.

"10 mins to go" Annette said to me, I finished the last of the white wine and lit another cigarette . . . . Then someone, somewhere shouted 5 mins to go. We were ushered into the interview booth, a tight squeeze for three of us. The interview started, I was asked so many questions, a lot of which I really didn't know the answers too. But remained professional and bluffed my way through it. They played Culture Club's single and also asked me if I would like a track played that I liked. I quivered for a bit and remembered driving from Ste Maxime to St Tropez and there was a song I had heard and loved. It was The Ballard of Lucy Jordan, by Marianne Faithful. Which they did. It kind of bought tears to my eyes. The interview over, they congratulated me as they had thought it had gone very well. They thanked us and gave us the gift of a bottle of Champagne. That wasn't bad way of earning £50 was it? We made our way back to Annette's Flat to share the Champagne and fortune with Katy and Milly. Going through the small narrow streets we heard some shouting and turned around, (we were kind of used to being harassed, but it usually was in a good way. They were shouting abuse and being very immature, and then started to throw ice lollies and ice creams at us, calling me a poof! (In French of course!) We just carried on and ignored them!! They continued to follow us back to Annette's. There was about 6 of them, still following and continuing to throw soggy melted ice and chocolate wafers!!

Annette slammed the keys into the apartment door, we closed the door quickly and ran upstairs. The youths were still outside shouting at us and throwing up the iced mess at the windows. Thank the Lord it wasn't bricks. We started throwing the ice back, it was sticky and yucky. We were having an "ice cream" fight with the local yobs!!! (God how pathetic.)

It all died down after about half an hour, some of the neighbours were shouting at us as well as the youths. It all went quiet, they must of got fed up and moved on. So we sat down for our evening meal of Spaghetti Bolognase and garlic bread, which the girls had cooked for us while we were at the radio. I shared out the cash a 100 Francs each. Money we were not expecting to by food and water on the journey to Dieppe.

We made our way to bed, as we were on our way to Dieppe the next day . . . or so we thought.

At 5am in the morning the very old French doors to Annette's apartment came crashing down . . . Literally!!!

It was the Police. We were arrested and handcuffed and thrown in a Police van and taken to the Police Station. (I still have no ideawhy they bought the police dogs with them?). So much for an early night! None of us had a clue why we had been arrested. One of the Police men had punched me in the face.

I was crying, I was scared and so was everyone. What the Hell had we done now??

Arrested and sent to Jail!

We had all been taken to the local police station, where we were ordered to strip off, out of all of our clothes bar our underwear. (It's one of those days you wish you were not wearing your grubbiest, tattiest old pants!). We were then bundled into two cells, Randy and I in one and the girls all together in the other. I was really scared, I hadn't a clue why we had been arrested, stripped and thrown into Jail! I mean I was only 15 years old and I don't think the cops realised this. It couldn't be legal, telling a kid to strip off and lock him into a cell. And our lack of French was so apparent. At least the girls had Annette to talk to the police. An officer came into our cell and gave us a plastic cup of water. He told us that we would be interviewed separately, I swear there was a smirk on his face. Time dragged by, it was at least an hour before they came back and took Randy away to be interviewed, then me and after that the girls, all one by one. They asked me "Who had?" through an interpreter about the ice cream and lolli's fight, and if I had broken into the ice cream kiosk?. I replied that I had not, and that I was being harrassed and called names in the street, by the French Youths and that they had followed us back to Annettes Apartment. I told them my age, but they seemed not in the least bit bothered. They just carried on smoking and looking at me in that smirking condescending way!

After about 5 hours they came back to the cell Randy and I shared and finally gave us our clothes back, and then told us we could ALL leave. (Thank the Lord!) We got dressed as if we were doing a quick change for one of the gigs, The girls stood in the foyer on the marble floor making noises with their shoes. Annette was engaged in a furious row with the policemen. Telling them how the French gang of youths were always walking up and down the main street causing trouble. But the police really didn't seem to care in the slightest. To them it had all jut been a bit of fun scaring the English weirdo's. Still smirking and smoking. I think that's all they knew how to do. They didn't appoligise or explain that we had been picked on. I asked one of them for a cigarette, he turned around to me and answered me in perfect English. "You, too young to Smoke!". And once again turned his back on me. In my head I shouted at "You arsehole wanker!". We grabbed up our bits and pieces and left the Cop Shop . . . we walked free from Jail. All I wanted to do now was go home . . . I hated the Police . . . . I hated France . . . I hated EVERYTHING!!!

We walked back to Annette's Flat and around 11am, we all decided enough was enough, we were too fed up to stay on for the few days with Annette. It was time for us to head back to England, time to make our way to Dieppe. Milly called Jimmy Jones in England and asked him about the tickets for our Ferry home. Which being the sweet guy he was, he agreed to help us out. He told her that the national press in the UK had been in touch with him about our infamous adventure in the South of France. Somehow the tabloids had heard about what I was up too! Maybe it was through the photographer, or the disco who knows? And to this day I still dont. When Milly told me, I was shocked, I think my mouth must of been open wide as my jaw dropped and hit the floor. That's all I bloody needed, more and more lies, and dressing up back in the UK . . . let alone the summer of it in France. What monster had I unleased, maybe I was getting paranoid and just dwelling on it too much.

We packed our bags for a final time, we thanked Annette for her friendship and hospitality, hugged and kissed, you know the cheek kissing French way and headed to the motoway. Annette told us that it shouldn't take too long if we were lucky with our lifts, we could be in Dieppe by night fall. She waved to us from her balcony, probably really angry that the gang had ruined the stay of her English friends. I was going to hitch with Randy this time, we were much closer after this summer. And Katy went with Milly. We arranged that each pair would get the ferry home and not wait for the others. It seemed silly to hang about for that. After all we would see each other once home. But it was a race to Dieppe we all wanted to get HOME! . . . The girls were picked up first . . . Typical . . . . it was another hour until we got our first lift.

The Madness Of Randy and I.

Eventually a car pulled up beside us, and the guy rolled down the window and asked us where we wished to go? . . . Home . . . I said in my head . . . all the way HOME!!! What we actually told him was near Paris as we were making our way to the port in Dieppe. He kindly obliged to take us some of the way and helped us in the car with our baggage. He was very nice looking if I remember correctly? He had very dark, deep, brown eyes and spoke to us in perfect English. We all chatted for ages, but at some point both Randy and I nodded off to sleep. Around 5.30pm the French Guy woke us up and showed us the motorway to go past Paris so we could be on our way to Dieppe. For late Summer it seemed so very hot, and the sun getting stronger and hotter ever second. He told us that there wasn't a service station for miles and kindly left us with a large bottle of water. If we were lucky we would catch the early eve rush hour traffic. And if we were really lucky. A lorry going all the way to Dieppe. We got a few short lifts, but found ourselves stuck in the blazing sun on the edge of the motorway.

We took it in turn to stand there with our thumbs out, while the other tried to nap on the roadside. We were so dehydrated, tired and emotionally Fucked up that we were so near, yet so far from HOME! We kept waking up confused not having a clue any longer where the hell we were? Lift after lift, without even looking at the map we jumped in and out of cars saying nothing but "Dieppe!???". It was getting dark, we had no idea where we were. I suddenly realised that in our last lift I had seen a sign on the motorway saying Le Harve. Yes you've guessed it we were going the wrong way . . . we were on the wrong side of the bloody motorway. We drank the last of our water, and sat there like 2 mad old dustbins! We had fucked up big time . . . . I lit another cigarette, grabbed our rucksacks told Randy to hold my hand and we dashed across the busy French motorway to the otherside . . . maybe now we would have some luck on getting to Dieppe. Well at least we were facing the correct direction now!

We had a couple more lifts, then a lift from a very sweet gay guy who wanted to take us for a drink . . . so we did. We were so thirsty. We were so tired and bewildered, not really with it at all. The guy was very friendly and was not after anything from us, unlike some of the nightmares of the journey down. We chatted best we could, almost dozing off at times. He told us we were actually quite near Dieppe, just a few KM's away.

"My God Randy! We've nearly made it!!" It had taken us about 11 hours, the gay guy gave us a little cash about £10 each, another earth angel, and told us to be careful and look after ourselves and kissed us on both cheeks. So sweet of him. He made us promise to eat and drink on the ferry. To be honest I had not thought about food or drink . . . only all I was imagining the ferry taking us over the channel, back to Newhaven. He shook our hands and thanked us for a pleasant evening. When he left, I turned to Randy and discussed how sweet and kind the guy had been, giving us money, when we had not been the most sparkling of company. Almost dozing off, slipping in and out of consiousness in the car let alone the gay club.

Suddenly from what seemed no where, we were so tired we had not even noticed this massive truck pull up beside us. "Where are you going? "we heard in an English accent. "Dieppe, PLEASE!" WE responded like 2 ragdolls, limp and lustless. "That's where . . . . we are going home!". The truck driver was friendly too he offered us some of his sandwiches, water and fags! Although it wasn't far to go, again we fell asleep. It seemed like only minutes, he awoke us to tell us we were here . . . ! We had finally reached Dieppe. We were a bit gushing when we thanked him, but we felt as if we had been rescued from a sinking ship.

Randy and I walked over to the ticket office and handed our passports over and when they handed them back . . . there were our ferry tickets inside. (Thank You Jimmy Jones!) The ferry was departing in 2 hours, So this meant we would arrive back in Newhaven by the early hours of the next morning.

We were allowed to board the ferry with the other passengers. We sat there starring at each other in complete disbelief, We were on board . . . we were REALLY going home!!! Was it a dream or an illusion in our altered state? I guess we then nodded off.

The sound of the Ferry's horn woke up Randy, I was so deeply asleep I never hears it, he had to shake me to wake me. He shouted too, and I woke with a start . . . "It's NEWHAVEN!!!" he squeeled. My madness was over . . . We were HOME!

We disembarked from the ferry and plodded like sheep following the crowd to the Train Station. Echoing through the tanoy was the anoccentment "The next train to Brighton is on time and will be arriving at Platform 2 in 15 minutes".

We are home! and off to Brighton. I dont remember much about the train home to Brighton, but I do remember that I was so overwhelmed by the excitement. We arrived at the station in Brighton very early, WE hugged and said see you later, Randy wandered up the hill home and I made my way to the bus stop to wait for the bus that would take me home to Saltdean.

Home to My Mum and Good Old Blighty,

I stood exhausted of all energy, leaning on anything, waiting for the bus to appear. It finally pulled up and I dragged my acheing body up the steps, plonked my tatty rucksack on the luggage rack. I had changed my few remaining francs in Newhaven so I had enough for the fare back to Saltdean.

The bus left Brighton station, the journey took me past the Palace pier, along the seafront, through Ovingdean, then Rottingdean where I just burst into tears. I was only five minutes from home and my Mum!

My stop was the saltdean Lido and I couldn't get off the bus quick enough and walked as fast as my sore legs would carry me. I knocked upon the door . . . "Mum! . . . Mum!" I yelled at the top of my voice. My Mum came out and grabbed me, and she took me in her arms and hugged me so tightly I felt I would either faint or explode into a million pieces. I WAS HOME, I WAS WITH MY MUM!!

I spent most of the day napping between telling Mum, the fun parts of my adventure. That Evening I sat smoking a cigarette gazing over the English Channel from our conservatory . . . contemplating the Summer in France . . . . I cried, I laughed, I felt ashamed, I felt overwhelmed. But I did it! I DID IT! . . . and what a Roller Coaster of a journey it had been . . . So many ups and downs. I made a decision there and then, I would never ever do that again. It was not safe, and now remembering and writing about it now in 2010, I realise how much worse it could of been. I was a mere child of 15, mind you at any age I dont think hitchhiking is something to do. The experience is very much alive in the hard drive of my mind, I will never forget what the group and myself went through that Hot, Sunny Summer in France . . . It was Mad, Crazy, and totally fabulous as well . . . If for one second I ever did think about doing it again . . . . I'd catch a flight and stay in a first class hotel.

Now I have relived my past, I shall light a cigarette and contemplate my future.

Until this very day I still do not know what ever happened to Zoe when she left me alone. We never actually ever spoke about it. I guess I'll just keep on guessing although I do have a vague idea!!!

DARON HOGG

Suzi Skelton